Privatisation and Private Higher Education in Kenya

PRIVATISATION AND PRIVATE HIGHER EDUCATION IN KENYA
Implications for Access,
Equity and Knowledge Production

Ibrahim Ogachi Oanda
Fatuma N. Chege
Daniel M. Wesonga

CODESRIA

Council for the Development of Social Science Research in Africa

© Council for the Development of Social Science Research in Africa, 2008
Avenue Cheikh Anta Diop Angle Canal IV, B.P. 3304 Dakar, 18524, Senegal
http://www.codesria.org

All rights reserved

ISBN: 2–86978–218-7
ISBN 13: 9782869782181

Typeset by Sériane Camara Ajavon

Cover image designed by Ibrahima Fofana

Printed by Imprimerie Saint Paul, Dakar, Senegal

The Council for the Development of Social Science Research in Africa (CODESRIA) is an independent organisation whose principal objectives are facilitating research, promoting research-based publishing and creating multiple forums geared towards the exchange of views and information among African researchers. It challenges the fragmentation of research through the creation of thematic research networks that cut across linguistic and regional boundaries.

CODESRIA publishes a quarterly journal, *Africa Development,* the longest standing Africa-based social science journal; *Afrika Zamani,* a journal of history; the *African Sociological Review; African Journal of International Affairs* (AJIA); *Africa Review of Books;* and the *Journal of Higher Education in Africa*. It copublishes the *Africa Media Review* and *Identity, Culture and Politics: An Afro-Asian Dialogue*. Research results and other activities of the institution are disseminated through 'Working Papers', 'Monograph Series', 'CODESRIA Book Series', and the *CODESRIA Bulletin.*

CODESRIA would like to express its gratitude to the Swedish International Development Cooperation Agency (SIDA/SAREC), the International Development Research Centre (IDRC), Ford Foundation, MacArthur Foundation, Carnegie Corporation, NORAD, the Danish Agency for International Development (DANIDA), the French Ministry of Cooperation, the United Nations Development Programme (UNDP), the Netherlands Ministry of Foreign Affairs, Rockefeller Foundation, FINIDA, CIDA, IIEP/ADEA, OECD, OXFAM America, UNICEF and the Government of Senegal for supporting its research, training and publication programmes.

Contents

List of Tables vii
Abbreviations and Acronyms viii
Acknowledgements ix
Note on contributors x

1. Introduction and Background of the Study 1

2. Evolution and Development of Private Higher Education in Kenya 19

3. Dynamics of Access and Equity in Kenya's Private Universities
   and Programmes 49

4. Research and Knowledge Production in Private Universities
   and Programmes in Kenya 76

5. Conclusion: Challenges and Prospects for Private Higher Education
   in Kenya as Regards Equity, Research and Knowledge Production 97

References 105

List of Tables

Table 2.0: Number and Status of private universities in Kenya, 2003 27

Table 2.1: Student enrolments in accredited private universities in Kenya 1996–1997 to 2002–2003 academic years 29

Table 3.0: Access and Admission requirements to four private universities in Kenya 54

Table 3.1: Public university admissions from disadvantaged (ASAL) regions as a percentage of the national intake 59

Table 3.2: Regional representations of students at CUEA 2003 60

Table 3.3: Average annual undergraduate tuition fees in private universities and programmes in Kenya 62

Table 3.4: Student enrolment by gender in public and private universities in Kenya: 1999/2000–2003/2004 67

Table 3.5: Competitive degree programmes in Kenyan public universities 72

Table 3.6: Key degree programmes in private universities in Kenya 73

Table 4.0: Degree granted by USIU by level: 2000–2004 89

List of Abbreviations & Acronyms

ASAL:	Arid and Semi Arid Lands
AVU:	African Virtual University
AICAD:	African Institute for Capacity Development
CHE:	Commission for Higher Education
CHIEA:	Catholic Higher Institute for East Africa
CUEA:	Catholic University of East Africa
HELB:	Higher Education Loan Board
GATS:	General Agreement on Trade in Services
IMF:	International Monetary Fund
IUCEA:	Inter-university Council of East Africa
IAVI:	International AIDS Vaccine Initiative
ICRAF:	International Centre for Research in Agriculture and Forestry
JAB:	Joint Admission Board
KAVI:	Kenya AIDS Vaccine Initiative
OECD:	Organisation for Economic Corporation and Development
SAPS:	Structural Adjustment Programmes
SES:	Socioeconomic Status
UEAB:	University of East Africa, Baraton
UNES:	University of Nairobi Enterprise Services
USIU:	United States International University

Acknowledgements

The members of the National Working Group (NWG) on higher education, Kenya, acknowledge the support they received from various individuals and institutions during fieldwork and writing of this report. The various respondents from the private and public universities who facilitated access to data for the research team deserve our sincere appreciation. The research team is also indebted to the students who availed their time for interviews and filing of questionnaires. The reviewers from CODESRIA made critical comments on the preliminary draft that guided the preparation and editing of the final manuscript. Our unreserved appreciation, deep gratitude and acknowledgement go to CODESRIA for funding the project. We however wish to absolve all the individuals and institutions mentioned above from responsibility for omissions and other interpreted errors in the report.

Notes on Contributors

Daniel Wesonga teaches Economics of Education and planning in the Department of Educational administration, Planning and Curriculum Development at Kenyatta University, Kenya. He has in the recent past coordinated a research project on the development of private universities in Kenya, commissioned by the Ford Foundation. Wesonga is also a member of Women Educational Researchers in Kenya (WERK), a private research organisation committed to research issues on women, gender and education.

Fatuma Chege teaches Philosophy and Sociology of Education in the Department of Educational Foundations, Kenyatta University Kenya. Her recent publications include: 'Constructing femininities and masculinities within the framework of domestic labour: the experience of Kenyan schoolchildren', in the *Journal of Educational Focus* (Lagos). She has also co-authored 'Sex talk and sex education' in the *African Journal of Aids Research*, and 'Gender sexual identities and HIV/AIDS Education in Africa', for UNICEF, East and southern Africa regional office (ESARO). Fatuma currently coordinates the Kenyan country study research project on African-Asian Universities Dialogue to Develop a Self-Reliant approach for Promoting Basic Education in Africa through Research; a joint undertaking by JICA, UNESCO, Hiroshima University and the Department of Educational Foundations, Kenyatta University.

Ibrahim Ogachi Oanda who coordinated this project and edited the final manuscript, teaches Sociology and Philosophy of Education at the Department of Educational Foundations, Kenyatta University, Kenya. His recent research includes 'Revitalizing Regional Collaboration in Higher Education and Training for Economic integration: The Case of the East African community (OSSREA)'. He has participated in research on 'The socioeconomic and regional profile of students in Kenyan public universities' (with Paul Achola), sponsored by the Ford Foundation, and with Okwach Abagi, 'Revitalizing the Financing of University Education in Kenya: Addressing strategies and wastage (AAU)'. Currently, Oanda is at the University of Illinois, Urbana-Champaign on post-doctoral research focussing on the teaching of Women and Gender Studies in East African Universities. He is also in the Kenya research team on the African-Asian Universities Dialogue to Develop a Self-Reliant Approach for Promoting Basic Education in Africa through Research.

1

Introduction and Background to the Study

Introduction

The emergence of private higher education in most of Africa in the last two decades has been one of the remarkable transformations related to the provision of higher education in the continent. In the main, the private higher education sector is small compared to traditional public provision. The forces that have led to the emergence of the sector in the continent are two-fold. Internally has been increasingly demand that the weak economies of African countries were unable to finance through public provision. At the international level, economic globalisation necessitated liberalisation of social service provision in individual countries and the subjection of demand and supply of such services to market logics. Higher education in Africa has increasingly been subjected to this market logic. This study analyses how the developments are affecting higher education provision in Kenya in respect to equity and knowledge production. These two tasks have traditionally been critical mandates that higher education was to contribute towards their achievement. The scope of the study is limited to the university sector of higher education. This sector has not only been the dominant, but also new entrants are exclusively interested in offering university level programmes. The study is presented in five sections. Section one conceptualises private higher education within the current discourse and then analyses the push factors for privatisation and private higher education in developing countries. The research issues that these developments have posed to higher education in Africa generally and Kenya in particular are raised within the context of this study. The second section reviews and profiles the evolution and historical development of private higher education in Kenya. Section three and four respectively analyse the effects of privatisation and private higher education on equity issues and research in Kenya. The last section discusses some challenges and prospects related to the growth of privatisation and private higher education in Kenya.

Conceptual and theoretical issues in privatisation and private higher education

In both the developed and developing countries, a new paradigm in the offering of higher education emerged from the 1980s. The emergence of the new paradigm was closely linked to a changed policy environment at a global level where government as the guarantor of public interest ceded control and ownership of capital to the private sector. Higher education was conceived crucial both in energising the transition from a public to a private sector-driven economy and in terms of producing the human capital required to consolidate the process. Before this paradigm change, higher education provision in most of the world was a public concern, in terms of both financing and function. Conceived as a post-war development strategy, countries continued to spend huge financial outlays in higher education systems to produce the human capital required for reconstruction. For example, up to the 1980s, 95 percent and 80 percent of students in Western Europe and the United States attended public universities respectively, while in Africa and Asia, public provision still continue to dominate the university sector (Varghese 2004).

The coupling together of the processes towards privatisation of public capital enterprises and higher education has altered the core focus of the mandates of higher education institutions. While the post war imperatives on which universities laid claim to public resources required that they execute their mandates in response to the needs of the wider public, privatisation requires that universities respond to the skill needs of private firms and individuals. This has been captured in the pressure for universities to teach 'market driven courses'. Such demands have led to changes in the traditional liberal curricula of universities. Skills in Business Administration and Information Technology have been the most sought-after, making universities compete for students in these areas, to the disregard of skill needs in other areas like medicine where developing countries face critical human capital shortages.

In most of Africa, the growth of privatisation and private higher education has been more a response to the global pressures than tangible internal policy forecasting to embrace private higher education. The pressures of globalisation and the inclusion of higher education in the World Trade Organisation's list of tradable goods target to open higher education markets in developing countries to strong established providers from the developed countries. Whereas higher education institutions in developing countries cannot compete with those of the developed countries in terms of the investments needed to make their higher education systems attract international students, the entry of strong private providers has began to radically alter the culture and practices of university institutions of Africa. Non-self supporting departments are being scrapped; introducing programmes based on their capacity to attract students and generate revenue, and the outsourcing of services have become common in African universities, and to the extent that no pause is, being made to relate these practices to the development needs of the countries.

In a discussion on the development of private higher education in Africa, Varghese (2004: 6-8) draws a distinction between privatisation of higher education and private higher education. Privatisation refers to the application of private sector or market principles in the operation and management of private higher education institutions while their ownership remains in the public realm. Privatisation can be partial or total depending on the degree to which the operation and management of the institutions have been ceded to private control. Most public universities in Africa have adopted the partial mode that has entailed introduction of partial tuition charges for students on public subsidy and mounting of parallel programmes where some students pay full tuition fees. Other universities have established private companies to run their income generating units and sold out catering and accommodation services to private entities. These developments are what have marked the privatisation of services, introduction of cost sharing and corporatisation of university management in most African countries.

Private higher education on the other hand indicates the growth of new higher education institutions that are wholly owned and operated by the private sector. This sector does not depend on any direct government funding for its growth and expansion. There are, however, cases where the government indirectly funds certain operations related to the regulation of the private institutions to protect the public interest. In Kenya, the operations of the Commission for Higher Education (CHE), which accredits and regulates the operations of private universities, are financed by the public. The government also provides tuition loans to students in private university institutions. As Varghese (2004) notes generally on Africa, and Levy (2003), specifically with regard to South Africa, private universities can take on diverse forms. The two types common in Africa are the 'for-profit' institutions and the 'not-for-profit' institutions. The 'not-for-profit' institutions, especially in the case of Kenya, are religious based institutions but integrate a secular curriculum in their academic programmes. The impression created is that the first types of institution operate to generate profit while the second charge to recover operating costs without realising a profit. However as this study will show, both institutions engage in market-like behaviour which entails the generation of profit. This position is indicated by the almost uniform amount of charges that both types of institutions levy for their services.

Privatisation and private higher education in Africa raise concerns related to how effective the private sector can be in executing the traditional mandates of higher education. Basically, the traditional role of universities can be categorised into three: the achievement of equity and the production of a high level workforce through teaching and learning; the development and application of new knowledge for the benefit of society through research, especially basic research; and the provision of public service to society (Mohamedbhai 1998). Ideally, public universities have been created on this logic. This is not to imply, however, that private higher education cannot encompass this function. It ideally depends on the extent that the logic of privatisation permits private higher education institutions to transcend social stratifications in their mandates.

Traditionally, as Adrianna Kezar (2004: 430) shows, the public role of higher education has focussed on educating citizens for democratic engagement. This entailed supporting local and regional communities, preserving knowledge and making it available to the community. This represented the social charter between higher education and society built on the communitarian philosophy of the public good. Transformations that have taken place from the 1980s have however introduced a new logic in the establishment of universities. The new logic emphasises the role of universities along the capitalist line of producing wealth and the success in earning it (Apple 1993). This latter logic, operationalised through the privatisation and marketisation of university education, leads naturally to the moral condemnation of those who fail to contribute to the production of profit. This logic has been applied in establishing private universities in most developing countries. The impetus for the application of the market logic in higher education has not been entirely the failure of public universities to respond to the traditional challenges, but rather, a response to changes in global capitalism. These changes have encouraged the entrepreneurial model of higher education where students are regarded as 'customers' and education a 'product'. The model makes universities good places for business, and requires less public funding. However, the implications for education may vary. These transformations may not necessarily be in consonant with the development challenges of developing countries, where increasingly, for profit higher education institutions are being established.

Privatisation and private higher education have been consequences of the broad influences of globalisation as a social, political and economic discourse. Underlying globalisation has been the neo-liberal argument about the role of the state in the economy, reduction of state expenditure, especially in subsidising social services, deregulation and liberalisation. Various practices and policies have been formulated in higher education institutions to have them conform to the new arrangements. These practices are referred variously as privatisation, commercialisation, marketisation, and corporatisation. All these terms put a premium on the organisational acumen of universities to generate their own operational costs and retain profit through engaging in business practices. Privatisation in higher education has therefore been marked by a gradual process of leaving the public sector of purely state supported services and moving towards greater self-sustainability (Johnson 2000:13).

With respect to Kenya, privatisation of higher education has taken four trajectories. The first has been the establishment of a variety of foreign and local private institutions to offer university level education. The second trajectory has been a variant of multi-nationalisation. This entails the linking of academic institutions or programmes of other countries with other institutions in Kenya. A student can be awarded a degree of a university in Australia, through a local institution that does not have a higher education 'status' but has entered into a twinning arrangement with the foreign university. The third is the investment of private resources often from corporate multinationals to fund and influence the nature of teaching and research both in public and private universities. The last and most controversial has been the semi-privatisation of public higher education institutions.

For developing countries, especially those in Africa, to benefit and participate in the new knowledge economy, their systems of higher education have to be more inclusive, and provide high quality training relevant to the needs of the local communities where they are located (Teffera & Altbach 2003, Mamdani 1993). Quality knowledge and training is a key component of competitiveness and crucial part of the country's development path. Since private universities, especially in Africa, have been established not in accordance with the public 'ideology' but that of the market, it is imperative to analyse how they respond to the challenges of national development. This is important because in several respects, the market logic goes against the developmental logic of the state. Preliminary studies from South Africa show that marketisation of university education and issues of equity are incompatible (Chachage 2001).

The practical operation of privatisation and private higher education differs from one country to the other depending on prevailing local conditions. Resources for investment in private higher education institutions can for example be generated from different sources. The origin and manner the resources are generated determine the direction the institutions develop in relationship to local issues affecting equity and knowledge production. Such resources can be provided by nationals and foreigners. The private sector can also denote an individual entrepreneur, a group of individuals or a private firm. The onus of a privatised higher education system is that public resources generated through taxation are not used to run these institutions, both in terms of financing recurrent and development expenditure nor in terms of being a source from where student can draw tuition support.

In discussing higher education privatisation, Ana-Maria Dima (2004) conceptualises the three concepts of deregulation, privatisation, and liberalisation as driving forces for globalisation within a local context. Deregulation and privatisation are conceived as forms of liberalising higher education markets (See also Dill 1997). By allowing private providers, governments have introduced higher education as a service on the market to be offered by those who seek profit and consumed by those who can comprehensively pay for it. The market rationale is a key logic in the liberalisation literature. Privatisation and liberalisation work in unison symbiotically speaking. Through liberalisation, a country permits providers other than the public to participate in offering higher education. It refers to a relaxation of various restrictions that limited the provision of higher education to the government. By liberalising therefore, a country logically privatises provision of higher education. Unlike privatisation that may be limited to nationals, liberalisation creates a scenario where foreigners can participate in providing education as a private good.

Privatisation however can be total or a question of degree. This is true of most developing countries that have vested public interests in public universities and have therefore resorted to gradual privatisation. Various degrees of private higher education do exist and as earlier noted, range from purely private institutions, to quasi-private ones. The difference in degree is often marked by the extent to which the private/public dichotomy is maintained. Where there is a degree of fusion in the responsibilities, then a situation of quasi-public, quasi-private occurs. For example in Kenya, students in private universities now qualify for a loan from a central kitty funded by taxpayers. The private students in public universities are taught by lecturers paid by the central government and treat payment from parallel students as overtime. Purely private universities without staff training programmes depend also on lecturers from public universities, most of who have been trained through forms of public sponsorship. A very independent self-regulating private higher education sector has not therefore emerged in Kenya although the private universities tend more towards pure privatisation.

In certain instances, privatisation of public universities has resulted to service provision by private firms. The University of Nairobi, the oldest and largest public university in Kenya, formed a private company that manages its private academic programmes and other income generating activities. All these are forms and scenarios of privatisation that exist in Kenya. Last is the idea of marketisation; a process of subjecting higher education provision to the economic rules that regulate buying and selling in the market place with profit maximisation as the overriding motivation. In this respect, institutions that offer additional services compete for clients, in this case students. Competition however is not the only market condition. The nature of expectation on the demand side conditions the type and quality of education services provided. One of the most cited reasons for privatisation and liberalisation of higher education in Kenya is that institutions are trying to respond to market expectations. In this age of globalisation, the market can take the form of national private firms, multinational corporations, state enterprises, and individuals. It is also likely that the expectations of the different market players can be divergent. In principle, this will necessitate a diversity of higher education institutions each responding to specific market niches or diversified programmes within individual institutions. In situations where institutional diversity has not occurred, then the issue is how individuals have to meet the various expectations.

Two issues are of concern as regards the marketisation of educational services. The first is related to the safeguards of the public interest, especially in instances where public universities have privatised and liberalised their programmes. Given the various players and the heterogeneity of the market, it is possible that universities as public institutions will respond to the interests of the private market forces — private firms, individuals and multinational corporations — and abandon the public service mission, or the public expectation from their operations. Put it another way, in the era of globalisation, higher education institutions may increasing satisfy the narrow, but influential interests of private corporations and individuals to the detriment of national development imperatives. The second issue and one that this study addresses is the type of knowledge produced in private degree programmes. Most academic programmes that are offered in privatised higher education systems are of the 'executive' type that emphasise applied as opposed to basic knowledge and trans-disciplinary as opposed to the compartmentalised knowledge forged by traditional higher education set-ups. The traditional research and dissemination functions of universities are increasingly overshadowed by short-term commissioned applied research and consultancies. In the developing country context, this means that higher education institutions are going to be conveyor belts of knowledge produced elsewhere, which may well be suitable to the functioning of the multinational corporation regarding profitability, but culturally inappropriate to the sustainability of local firms.

The present study therefore conceptualises privatisation, liberalisation and marketisation as nation-state policies and practices that energise the processes of globalisation and internationalisation of education. The key concern is what extreme processes of globalisation will imply for higher education in developing countries like Kenya. Developing countries do not have strong universities of international repute to attract large numbers of tuition-paying international students. They also may not boost enormous indigenous capital that can be invested in private higher education. This means they will be net importers and consumers of education services from the western countries. Countries like Kenya have more than half of their population living below the poverty line. This population is unlikely to benefit from higher education offered on the market. These concerns cause reflection on the issue of whether globalisation and privatisation of higher education may not turn into the neo-colonialism of the twenty-first century (Altbach 2004).

From public to private higher education in developing countries

From the time of their inception, a marked feature of higher education institutions in developing countries was their structure and stature as public institutions. This situation still obtains to some degree at the level of financing and administration. Such features of higher education provision were not, however, unique to developing countries. They are a historical tradition that European colonialism transplanted to the colonies. To this extent therefore, the European model of a university, as a public institution tasked with a public responsibility, was institutionalised as a universal phenomenon. In most parts of the developing world, more especially in Africa, the European model of higher education provision largely reigns. This is manifested by the volume of public supported students in public, and of late, private universities, though such government subsidies have been declining. The public responsibility of the European model university, and therefore, the basis of their claim to public resources, is grounded in their task of providing training in specialised areas. They act as niches for discovery and transmission of new knowledge and as avenues for socialisation in social and political values. Such responsibilities provide parameters for gauging the relevance of universities to society, be they public or private.

Conceptually, higher education comprises various post-secondary education and training institutions. In Kenya, the institutions include a range of middle level colleges. These colleges are important training grounds for vocational skills. They feed the economy with a workforce equipped with skills that do not require the long-term professional training as is given at the universities. The extent to which these colleges have been affected by privatisation of higher education is varied. There are those that were quasi-private such as the Harambee Institutes of Technology established by community efforts. Others, such as the training institutions under various ministries, were purely public. Yet others were purely private, run by either religious bodies and or private concerns. Kenya also has four national polytechnics. These are at Mombasa, Nairobi, Eldoret and Kisumu. They offer academic programmes up to the Higher National Diploma level. The polytechnics have resisted attempts to suck them into the national university system but want to evolve to university level institutions on their own. The middle level institutions have however been sucked into the privatisation frenzy through mechanisms of accreditation, collaboration and twinning programmes with public and foreign private universities. The many colleges constitute the non-university sector of higher education in Kenya. The focus of this study does not include this non-university sector. It is limited to the public and private degree-awarding universities in the country. This is because of their status in terms of setting trends in higher education.

The model of a pure public higher education system, more in terms of financing but less in its function, has been eroded over time. The reasons for these are not exclusively limited to financial explanations. Universities serve social, economic and political purposes. The logic of internationalisation towards the end of the twentieth century dictated that such ends could be better served if knowledge production and dissemination were managed as a private enterprise. In the developed world, trends towards private initiatives in the provision and management of higher education institutions grew alongside the expansion of the industrial middle class in the nineteenth century and the acceptance of private enterprise as a driving force for economic development. The history of the establishment and operation of universities in these countries is long. Universities here have grown into diverse and complex institutions. There are systems of pure public and pure private universities with varying degrees of public support in the continuum. These ensure that their responsibilities converge to the extent that they contribute to greater public good regardless of their sources of funding. In the developing countries, especially those of sub-Saharan Africa, universities are still few compared to social demand. Institutional diversity is also limited as much as sources of their funding. It is not therefore possible to establish universities in terms of specialisations as either purely teaching or purely research institutions. Even when they have been set up as private institutions, the expectations have been that they strike a balance between teaching, research and public service. These are the expectations that made most African countries reluctant to embrace private higher education in earnest.

Privatisation of higher education gained momentum in most of Africa from the 1990s. This was due to circumstances that the political elite could not circumvent. These circumstances were both internal and external. The internal dynamics relate to the increased demand for access to higher education, and the lack of expansion of higher education institutions. Demographic and developmental imperatives fuelled a desire for increased access from hitherto excluded groups, and the continued expectation for higher education to provide trained personnel for economic development (Banya 2002, World Bank 2000). Having achieved mass primary and secondary education in the 1970s and during part of the 1980s, the political elite in Africa had to expand higher education as part of fulfilling the dreams of independence.

Concomitantly, those who had gone through mass primary and secondary education had come of age and wanted more education at higher levels for social mobility. In the Kenyan context, the number of students admitted to universities under government sponsorship, and the increase in the number of public universities from one institution at independence to five in the early 1990s, was often cited by the political leadership as a credit to their nationalist vision.

The perceived role of higher education in socioeconomic development, particularly, justified government funding of university expansion (Altbach 1992). For their part, universities were expected to reciprocate by providing advanced education, fostering research and scientific development, and participating in the creation and transmission of knowledge through research networks (Saint 1992, UNESCO 1998). These mandates became the yardstick by which relevance and the quality of higher education was measured. Expansion in the number of public university institutions and the volume of students was however short-lived. In the 1970s, both internal and external factors influenced continued investment in and expansion of higher education. Internally, universities were seen as key to the development of work force resources and knowledge needed for the development of the new nations. Externally, the idea of the university as a focus for socioeconomic development received financial support from international organisations, notably the World Bank and OECD countries. However, this optimism waned in the 1980s. The economic crisis discussed of this decade saw public recurrent expenditure per university student fall from US$6,461 in 1975 to US$2,365 in 1983 (Samoff & Carrol 2003). From the mid-1980s, most African economies were too weak to support any expansion of public institutions and even to support existing ones efficiently.

The weak position of sub-Saharan African countries should be understood within a context, which for purposes of this study had a direct impetus for the growth of private, higher education. The context was the world economic recession of the 1980s that was occasioned by the 1973 'oil shocks' and the collapse of the international coffee agreement in 1989. The rise in the price of oil forced African countries into borrowing from the international market to meet internal shortfalls. The collapse of the coffee agreement that had controlled coffee marketing reduced the price of coffee — a major source of foreign exchange earnings. The resulting balance of payments deficit led many countries to increase external borrowing, and hence more debt. By the mid-1980s the option for most of these countries was to default in payments, or to implement Structural Adjustment Programmes (SAPS) developed by the International Monetary Fund (IMF) to continue servicing their debts. For the international community, the African problem was diagnosed not as economic but political. This political problem was rooted in the workings of the one-party state. It was in attempts to cling to a one-party structure in the face of the insistence of western donors to dismantle it that quality higher education and other social services became casualties. While African governments reduced funding to higher education to beef up their political structures, donors diverted funds to institutions and groups that best contributed and manifested their values of 'good governance'.

Donor support for education in Africa in the 1990s was most concentrated in primary education. This was influenced by World Bank studies that now argued that investment at the lower levels of education generated more social returns than higher education whose returns were to the individual. These assertions caused a rethinking in policies for education support among traditional donors. The view that higher education in Africa benefited a few privileged students from elite backgrounds began to circulate. Arguments that resources spent on higher education did not rationally justify the economic criteria of social efficiency began to gain currency among donors. This climaxed during the 1990 world conference on education for all, where investment in basic education was touted to have higher rates of social return compared to higher education. In most of the 1980s and 1990s therefore, donor support to higher education in Africa was substantially reduced. Unfortunately, this was at a time when African economies were increasingly weak due to the consequences of SAPS, and the social demand for access to higher education was so high. Alternatives to address the demand for increased access to higher education had to be sought. Students in higher education institutions also became increasingly entangled in the political and social struggles of their countries, often supporting the opposition to governments of the day. This made governments view them as a threat to stability, rather than as an economic investment they were thought to be at independence. This confluence of internal economic weaknesses, social demand and changing international politics accelerated the development of private higher education. The fact that private institutions entered the scene when the attention of existing governments was focussed on political survival meant that mechanisms of surveillance were lacking. For example in Kenya, although the CHE had been established back in 1985 to oversee the development in the private university sector, this mandate was only officially spelt out in 1989. The operations of CHE as will be seen later have not been backed by adequate government legislation to date, especially with regard to the privatisation of higher education in public institutions.

The other external forces are those that constellate around the process of globalisation. Conceptually, globalisation has been marked by the massive developments in communication and technology, the restructuring of global capitalism, the collapse of the Soviet Union and the end of the Cold War during the last decade of the twentieth century. This development set in motion economic and social trends that stressed profits and market-driven policies as the new centres of power and influence. The trends have come to affect structures through which higher education was offered; the public logic within which higher education was traditionally offered was dissipated in favour of a market-driven private logic as the more efficient model for higher education. Private sector ideas and business practices have been entrenched in publicly funded higher education institutions. Global privatisation, quasi-marketisation and corporate managerial practices increasingly characterise the higher education sector in most countries now (Ntshoe 2003). The overriding principles of globalisation have been in the weakening of the state, the questioning of the tenets of the welfare state, especially with regard to its efficiency in providing social services, and the adoption of a corporate culture in the provision of such services.

Concerning developing countries, globalisation is associated with international competition in the provision of higher education and increasing internationalisation (co-operation) between countries, systems, institutions and individuals in its provision. It is in this respect that cross-border and transnational education have become the major purveyors of globalisation values. These values entail the application of market fundamentals in the provision of higher education and institutional, organisational and behavioural changes that facilitate the commoditisation of their knowledge production capacities. At the level of individual nation states, globalisation has forced a kind of paradigm shift in the manner that higher education has traditionally been provided. This shift has been of concern to developing countries. Douglass (2005: 6) has characterised this shift to include among others, the following: the rise of non-traditional for-profit and not-for-profit competitors to provide higher education, the repositioning of existing institutions into new markets driven by the desire to generate operational revenues and achieve cost savings, and change in the recruitment markets for students and faculty. The demand for academic programmes by students is motivated by their need to seek the academic quality and credentials of programmes offered by certain universities, or simply a desire for a different cultural experience.

Certain assumptions underlie the logic of globalisation. Kwiek Marek (2003: 19) groups these into three. First, there is the alleged collapse of the role of the nation state in social and economic development and of its vision of higher education as a treasure contributing to national consciousness. Second, there has been the reformulation of the functions of the welfare state, including a diminished scope of public sector activities to be funded by the state. Third, there has been the invasion of notions of economic rationality and corporate culture into social service provision worldwide. In the field of higher education, globalisation has occasioned a rethinking in the provision of higher education as a public good. The idea has been that since higher education services derive more private than social benefits it would be more socially efficacious if they were offered to those who could afford to pay for them. This logic has led to the increased privatisation of higher education institutions and programmes. Global internationalisation and multi-nationalisation of academic programmes have become critical avenues through which the privatisation of higher education has been induced in developing countries. Through this avenue, adaptations of academic programmes or institutions from one country to another become more prevalent (Altbach 2004). The consequent result has been the growth of private universities and the involvement of private interests in determining access and curricula as opposed to public interests. The offering of university education on market principles raises issues on how the 'university' has to carry out its traditional public mandate and act as a mechanism of achieving equity and socioeconomic development. This is especially so in developing countries where social and economic differentiation is an obstacle to overall development.

The influence of globalisation in the private provision of higher education has been deepened through the inclusion of higher education as a tradable good by the World Trade Organisation (WTO). The WTO seeks to include education as one of the internationally traded services and to reduce national control over its regulation. In these respect there are negotiations to enact legislation such as the General Agreement on Trade in Services (GATS), to regulate the commercial exchange and trade in educational services (Altbach 2001, Knight 2003). The aim of GATS is to facilitate the import and export of educational services and institutions as private economic concerns. These developments have implications for the quality and relevance of private higher education offered in developing countries. Issues related to quality assurance, accreditation and recognition of credentials are subsumed under the logic that what comes from the 'international' market is good and relevant for developing countries. The broad implications of what GATS may mean for higher education systems in developing countries have not been fully examined. Indeed systems for the internationalisation, liberalisation and privatisation of higher education serve as the driving forces for this process, as they do for globalisation. As Douglass (2005:7) speculates, the application of GATS to higher education may rule out state subsidisation of public higher education as an infringement on free markets. Besides, such subsidisation would need to be extended to other private for-profit institutions. Aspects of this process are already happening in Kenya. Private universities have successfully lobbied for their students to receive tuition loans from the government. They are also campaigning to be considered for other government subventions like those extended to public universities. This is besides the indirect benefits they access such as teaching staff that have already been trained through public subsidies.

Indeed traffic in commercial private education is one-way, both in terms of the net flow of students and ownership of the profits generated. Even when private institutions from developed countries are established in developing countries, the tendency has been to offer their curriculum using the term 'international' as a brand to market their courses. This is not entirely bad. However if private institutions and programmes do not include content that is specific to the development challenges of developing countries, then they deepen processes of alienation and dependency. As Knight (2003:10) reveals, the rationale for importing or exporting, education services does not place developing countries at any advantage. The developed world has the capacity to both import and export. The rationales for importing include:

- limited domestic capacity to meet growing demand for higher education;
- provision of greater access to specific knowledge or skills based education and training;
- improvement of the quality of higher education provision by allowing market access to prestigious foreign institutions;
- the creation of a culture of political alliances; and
- the development of human capital and stemming the brain drain;
- the rationale for exporting on the other hand includes:
- excess national capacity in higher education;
- income generation;
- strategic cultural, political and economic alliances;
- institutional strengthening and innovation;

- a tool for further internationalisation of domestic institutions; and
- using education as a conduit to access trade in other services.

The cumulative impact of the foregoing developments has made the privatisation of public higher education and the growth in private universities issues that raise concern regarding the relationship of higher education to national objectives. Most countries of sub-Saharan Africa, perhaps with the exception of South Africa, have not been inserted into the global education market as equals. Of concern are fears that unfettered privatisation of higher education will erode the little capacity in national higher education systems and once again force African countries to spend scarce resources for overseas training of their work force. Hence, while the arguments propelling privatisation of higher education in Africa are persuasive, private higher education may turn out to be more expensive ultimately to the public if national development objectives are not qualitatively addressed by the sector. This is in instances where such education would lead to poor quality skill development among workers. Given Africa's peripheral position in global development, the privatisation and marketisation of higher education therefore leads to a questioning of the logic of the market. Markets assume perfect homogeneous conditions where clients are not only free to choose but also have equal capacity to benefit from what the market offers. Market rationality also assumes diversity in the products offered and opportunity structures to exercise the skills so gained. As will be argued in this study diversity in terms of the curriculum of private universities in most of Africa is a still limited.

The considerations above continue to pose challenges given the extent to which private higher education has been embraced in Africa. The challenges revolve around the traditional role of university education that characterised universities as institutions that promoted the wider public interest in the process of knowledge production and utilisation. This public interest role has been defined from the perspective of the wider society to which individual and institutional efforts are embedded and directed. The role of the university in this regard is evaluated concerning its contribution to social development, social justice and democratic engagement (Newman 2000, Kezar 2004, Rhoades, undated). The mandate of the university therefore to serve a public good and interest should be manifested in institutional commitment to national development, questions of access, equity, commitment to quality of the knowledge generated, and modes of instruction (Olukoshi & Oyekanimi 2001; Altbach 1992). Private higher education offered on the neo-liberal logic of market rationality is unlikely to address the public interest so conceived. This is because the neo-liberal logic re-conceptualises the public interest in terms of individual rights, in the belief that a weak state is better than a strong one and that what is private is necessarily good and what is public is necessarily bad (Apple 2001).

The stress on individual choice and the market forces institutions and faculty to focus too much on short-term revenue generating activities. This can be detrimental to institutional commitment to broader, more long-term and long-standing educational, social ,scholarly and public service functions (Bok 2003, Rhoades, undated).This is to the extent that the neo-liberal paradigm, whether presented as privatisation, commercialisation, or corporatisation, has affected all aspects of the university enterprise, including teaching, research and service (Zeleza 2003:165).

Privatisation and private higher education in Kenya: Research issues

The key research issues that the development of private higher education in developing countries raise are related to the logic of their operations and how they rationalise their operations in the context of the knowledge needs of society. The global surge for private higher education institutions is partly related to the emerging diversity of students and the skill needs of the 'globalising' economy. Private universities and programmes are mostly self-financing and this means they have to focus on students who are able to pay tuition fees. These operational imperatives necessitate that private universities operate more autonomously with respect to the kind of students they admit and the nature of the courses they offer. The orientation has been to offer vocational courses that are not capital intensive. In an era when the demands of the global knowledge economy require huge capital investments in research for national competitiveness, the focus of private universities in applied courses and programmes seems to place the societies where they operate at a disadvantage. This is more worrisome in countries like Kenya where private higher education may be able to enrol more students compared to those in public universities and programmes.

The development of private higher education in Kenya started just before independence. Three phases have dominated their evolution. The first phase that started at independence was marked by the development of middle level, non-degree religious institutions. The institutions that developed then as higher education institutions were not of university status. They were colleges that were set up by religious organisations for the purpose of training their clergy. Some of these institutions included St Paul's Theological founded in 1930, the Kenya Highlands Bible College in 1953, and the African Inland Mission's Scott Theological College in 1962. There were also secular private vocational colleges that developed after independence such as the Kenya Institute of Management. These colleges focussed on training for vocational skills especially in Commerce, Accountancy and Business Education.

The second phase started from the 1980s through to the 1990s. During this phase, there was a growth in demand for university education in the country. However, expansion of public universities was slow as resources from the government were dwindling. Attempts to increase intake to the few public universities led to congestion and serious erosion in the quality of programmes. It was during this period that some of the religious and secular colleges that had been established during the first phase were transformed into degree-awarding institutions and were given university status. These were the United States International University (USIU) established in 1970, the University of East Africa Baraton (UEAB) in 1978, Daystar Communications in 1974, and the Catholic Higher Education Institute of East Africa (CHEIA) in 1983. The last phase dates from the mid-1990s. This phase has been marked by the expansion and semi-privatisation of public universities, the expansion of private universities and an aggressive competition for students between all of these entities.

The Kenya government, in recognition of its inability to continue subsidising public universities, laid the foundation for the growth of private universities in the 1980s. A presidential commission that worked on mechanisms for establishing a second public university recommended the setting up of a council to regulate the growth of private higher education in Kenya. Such a council was set up in 1985, and was known as the Commission for Higher Education (CHE). The CHE however did not begin this task immediately because of government reluctance to privatise university education. However, due to pressure from donors and the growing number of applicants who were unable to secure places in public universities, CHE formally published rules for establishing and registering private universities in 1989. The activation of CHE's activities, the growing social demand and the loss of confidence in the poorly financed public universities, facilitated the development of private higher education.

At the time of the study, there were six chartered private universities, six registered private universities, and five operating with letters of interim authority. The accredited Universities category comprised UEAB, CUEA, USIU, Daystar University, Scott Theological College and African Nazarene University. The registered universities were the East African School of Theology, Kenya Highlands Bible College, and Nairobi Evangelical Graduate School of Theology, Nairobi International School of Theology, Pan African Christian College and St Paul's United Theological College. These institutions offered degrees even before the advent of CHE but have still not satisfied the requirements for accreditation as university institutions. The third category operating under letters of interim authority were established after the establishment of CHE. They are Kenya Methodist University, Kabarak University, Kiriri Women's University of Science and Technology, Agha Khan University and Strathmore University. These institutions come to a total of 17 private universities operating, despite their different levels of official recognition – a fast growth in a period of about ten years. The 17 private universities supplement the six existing public universities.

The rapid growth of private universities was facilitated by responsive government policy that came into being in 1991. This was a policy negotiated between the government and donors to enable the release of an adjustment credit that the country needed to revamp the public university system. The government's education adjustment policy focussed on mechanisms of expanding enrolments in higher education as a way of serving equity objectives by opening access to students from a wider range of socioeconomic backgrounds (Wandiga 1997). The issue of broadening access and equity were therefore central to the government's recognition of private universities. Encouragement of private universities was also aimed at diffusing pressure away from public universities and at addressing national work force imbalances. In addition to the private universities, the government encouraged public universities to start income generating projects to supplement government subsidies. This has led to the introduction of parallel (private) degree students in all the public universities. The parallel students are admitted separately from the regular students, pay fees at market rates and sometimes have lectures separate from the regular students. Their admission criteria are also much more flexible, in terms of previous academic qualifications, than the regular students. This scenario has resulted in the semi-privatisation of public universities in Kenya. The full private universities and the parallel (private) students in public universities therefore constitute the privatised market system of university education in Kenya.

There have been varying views on the capacity of the privatised market system to address the challenges of university education in Kenya. One view holds that private universities are of higher quality than public ones, are better organised, and have played a significant role in offsetting the demand for university education in Kenya (Mwiria & Ngome 1998, Murunga 2001). There are also studies that have interrogated private higher education in relation to the traditional responsibilities of universities. Such studies note tendencies towards social exclusion of those who are unable to pay, stratification of the scholarly community, a weakening of their collective capacities, the demeaning of academic freedom and a deterioration in quality (Chacha 2002, Zeleza 2003). Other views have been more dismissive, seeing private universities as offering narrow and irrelevant curricula, and having fewer beneficial implications for the socioeconomic development of the country.

The above views have not been conclusively interrogated. Even where field data exist, there has been a tendency among university administrators to go on the defensive, in order to sustain their market niche. This is due to the competition for students between private universities themselves, and between private universities and the public and private degree programmes. In the case of Kenya, the introduction of parallel programmes has made the role of CHE in enforcing quality standards more difficult. Public universities are rather insulated from strict adherence to some quality assurance measures. This is because as long as they generate money and take away the pressure for budgetary support from the government, the government is likely to turn a blind eye to reported malpractices. These are the perceptions that have made private universities complain more often that CHE is unfairly strict on them. It may be that some of the claims being made about the attractiveness of programmes and the innovativeness of the new institutions are just marketing labels. Potentially, this conceals the total picture about the viability and implications of privatising higher education in developing countries.

It must be noted that there was a period of about ten years in Kenya when private universities operated exclusively without competition from the public universities. This was when admission to public universities was highly restricted. However, from the time public universities relaxed admission criteria and started admitting private students, studies have not been conducted to document the trends regarding access and expansion in the private universities. This is important if the claims of private universities to offer attractive, high quality programmes are to be validated and sustained. Besides, the views do not touch on the core mandate of universities; that is achieving equity through broadening of access to all social groups, promoting indigenous knowledge systems through research and dissemination, and producing relevant personnel for socioeconomic development of the country. The present study addresses the above issues as they relate to the operations of private universities, and to the introduction of semi-private programmes in Kenya's public universities.

The present study takes the position that systems of higher education have to be evaluated based on their responsiveness to a country's development imperatives. In the case of Kenya, such imperatives were pointed out by the Presidential Commission that looked into the establishment of the second university back in 1984. The commission stressed the importance of systems of higher education that focussed on scientific and technological disciplines, rural development, cultural values, and environmental issues. Indeed even at a global level, these are key issues that merit the attention of policy makers in relation to education. Studies should therefore provide indicators regarding the extent to which private higher education has been able to alleviate the problems of access, equity, and relevance better than public higher education. This study has attempted to address the above issues. The impact that privatisation and private higher education has had on access, equity and production of knowledge was thus part of the analysis.

Providing knowledge on these issues is important as university education remains an important vehicle for socioeconomic development, and therefore attracts much public interest. This public interest should obtain and be manifested in the structural workings of private universities. The study focussed on policies of access and admission and the research orientations of programmes in the private universities, and the public universities' 'private' degree programmes. Three broad objectives guided this study. These were:

- To provide an analysis of factors contributing to privatisation and the growth of private higher education in Kenya;
- To analyse the degree to which private universities and programmes addressed the issues of equity through various access policies;
- To analyse the extent to which privatisation and private higher education have enhanced or limited the functions of the university related to research, knowledge production, and dissemination.

Methodological orientation of the study

Data related to the evolution of privatisation and private universities in Kenya were collected through a critical review of the literature and through interviews with key respondents. Detailed information related to access and knowledge production was collected from four private universities and two public universities. The private universities were the United States International University (USIU), University of East Africa, Baraton (UEAB), Catholic University of East Africa (CUEA) and Daystar University. The four universities were chosen as they are the oldest in terms of private higher education provision and have higher student numbers. Nairobi and

Kenyatta Universities were chosen as case studies with regard to trends in the privatisation and liberalisation of public higher education in Kenya.

Three key instruments were used to collect data for the study. These were historical analysis of trends, survey questionnaires, supplemented with structured interviews, and the analysis of documents. Records related to the foundation and development of private higher education in Kenya were analysed. The analysis was useful in identifying the forces that have shaped their growth. Two types of questionnaire were utilised for the study. The first was a student questionnaire that was used to map the socioeconomic profile of students in private universities and in private degree programmes in public universities. The second type of questionnaire was administered to faculty deans and academic registrars in the various universities and programmes. The information from these instruments was supplemented by structured interviews of a sample of students and university administrators. These interviews were aimed at establishing admission criteria of students, policies of access and equity, tuition and other charges, and issues related to faculty research activities. Analysis of documents in the various programmes was carried out, especially with respect to research issues and protocols. The idea was to establish trends in research pursuits in private universities and degree programmes in public universities. The budgets of the universities, where these were available, were analysed to establish allocations for research and student financial aid schemes. This information has been interrogated in the light of the mission statements of the various universities to determine the direction in which privatisation is influencing research in higher education institutions.

Conclusion

The privatisation of public universities and the emergence of private higher education pose challenges to the role of university education in Kenya. On one hand, these challenges relate to the degree to which privatised institutions can address broad social issues such as equity and knowledge production. On the other hand is the dissonance of the legal status of private higher education institutions and the commercial zeal that underlies their operations. Another issue relates to the high demand for university places that drove the emergence of the private higher education sector and the percentage of qualified students that the sector absorbs annually. The subsequent sections of this study interrogate these challenges and their influence on access, equity and research mission of universities in Kenya.

2

Evolution and Development of Private Higher Education in Kenya

The idea of higher education as a public concern in Kenya

As in the case of most developing countries that were colonised, nationalist passions contributed immensely to the emergence and character of higher education in Kenya. The first public university in the country, the University of Nairobi, was set up in 1970, when the University of East Africa, at Makerere, Uganda, was de-established. Post-independence nationalism among the three East African countries of Kenya, Uganda and Tanzania accelerated the break-up of the federal university arrangement in favour of national public universities for each of these countries.

From the period of its inception, the University of Nairobi owed its existence to public resources. As a nationalist institution, the University undertook the responsibility for political socialisation, an ideological endeavour to reconstruct the political thinking of Africans to support the ideals of African socialism as a foundation for nation building. Indeed, both the nationalists and the colonial government collectively pursued the appetites for higher education in the colonies and the decolonisation process, albeit with different aims. In Kenya, it was the nationalist surge and racial tensions occasioned by the Mau Mau revolt that forced the colonial administration to consider the need for higher education in the country. After independence, expansion of higher education systems in the country accelerated to meet the continued demand from Kenyan Africans for such training. At the same time, the government used higher education as an avenue of training indigenous personnel for its Africanisation process, itself a political endeavour.

There were, however, other considerations for the 'public orientation' of higher education besides politics. Economically, higher education was considered crucial in modernising independent Kenyan society. It was therefore thought prudent to spend public resources since it was considered that in the long term the whole country stood to benefit through the application of skills to transform society. Generally, the drive to provide higher education was informed by three assumptions that prevailed at the time on a worldwide scale regarding the role of higher education for national development (Farrell 1992:107). The assumptions were that: (a) it led to the generation of more wealth within a nation (economic development); (b) the more equitable distribution of such wealth or opportunity to access such wealth increased with the more the people who accessed high education (social development); (c) higher education contributed to political socialisation and democratisation on a scale that approximated development in western Europe (political development).

The above considerations meant that the public had to finance higher education, but that institutions offering such education could claim a measure of autonomy to regulate their internal affairs. In return, the public could look to the universities to provide answers to socioeconomic and political problems. The overriding logic then was that higher education carried too great a critical responsibility to be left to operate without public accountability or remain in private hands. The government too by virtue of its position as the planner and executor of economic programmes was best placed to determine the priorities for the university, such that university development was well articulated with national development plans.

There is one aspect of higher education development in Kenya related to this study that needs to be pointed out. Unlike Tanzania and Uganda which leaned towards socialist ideologies after independence, Kenya leaned towards the capitalist path. Hence whereas in Tanzania and Uganda nationalist party policies were institutionalised in university life, higher education in Kenya tended to be elitist from the beginning and operated on a laissez faire basis that allowed the operation of market forces to some extent. For example, in Tanzania, admission of students to university took into account an attestation of character from the village party leader and performance in pre-university compulsory national service, besides performance in school certificates (Ajayi et al. 1996). This was not the case in Kenya. Access to university education was secured through competitive examinations as the only consideration.

Two observations can be derived from these points. One, the idea of offering higher education as a marketable good was ingrained in Kenyan society right from independence when the country leaned towards capitalism as a basic mode of socioeconomic organisation. Indeed, as will be shown shortly, the pressure to expand high education had been occasioned by private resources that had been expended in expanding primary and secondary education in the country in the 1970s and 1980s. In fact, two private university institutions were operational in Kenya from the 1970s. The first was the United States International University (USIU), which opened a small campus in Nairobi in 1970. The second was the Baraton University of East Africa that began in 1980. The readiness to offer higher education on market principles later saw the steady growth of private higher education institutions from the mid-1980s. This steady growth was not paralleled in any other country in the East and Southern African region, besides the Republic of South Africa. At face value, this is an impressive development given global trends towards privatisation. This shows that the threshold for the private provision of higher education was established at independence given the development paradigm that the country adopted. The issue that needs further analysis is the impact this development has had on equity.

The second observation relates to higher education and its public function. Irrespective of the fact that private resources have been expended in developing higher education institutions, they are still expected to execute a public mandate. In fact, the very acceptance and growth of higher education institutions has been a demand from the public for more access. The public interest in private higher education institutions does not therefore just disappear because they are private. There is a degree, in fact a higher degree, of government involvement in private higher education provision. The forms of knowledge that are produced and disseminated from such institutions have therefore to meet the broad expectations of the 'public' first as a key market before other considerations are raised. This public/private mix has to be taken into consideration when analysing the implications of privatisation and marketisation in knowledge production. The basis for evaluating how relevant private higher education institutions are engaging in knowledge production, is first to establish the knowledge needs of a country.

The development paradigm that Kenya adopted at independence implicitly determined the nature and character of higher education. The ideology of African socialism, as articulated in Session Paper No. 1 of 1965 concerning development planning, aimed to create a spirit of a communitarian approach to capitalist development. In this sense, the idea of expending private resources to provide social services was rooted in the Kenyan society. However, at the same time, the encouragement of market forces in socioeconomic life created an elite class that could accelerate the development of local private enterprise and create the demand for services offered outside the public realm. The 1960s and 1970s therefore laid the threshold conditions for the evolution of private higher education in Kenya.

The demand for and regulation of private higher education in Kenya

Towards the 1980s, the pressure for university education, and therefore the need for its expansion, intensified in Kenya. The increased demand for university education was a consequence of policies the government had pursued in the education sector from independence. Given the racial and inequitable manner in which education was provided before independence, the government had a moral responsibility to redress such imbalance. In the primary education sector, a series of government policies were initiated to achieve universal primary education. Such policies entailed a waiver of direct parental and community contributions to schools in the form of school fees and the introduction of school feeding programmes in the semi-arid and arid districts of the country. Secondary school places were also expanded through government financial support, and community mobilisation in the form of 'Harambee', a communal pulling together of resources to provide services such as education. The net result of this development was an increase in the number of students who sought access to post-secondary higher education institutions in the 1980s.

The expansion that had taken place at the only public university, the University of Nairobi, had not kept pace with the developments sketched above. The number of new entrants to the university had grown from 565 undergraduates and 306 postgraduates during the 1970–1971 academic year to 7,478 undergraduates in the 1980–1981 academic year. The growth in student numbers also had two consequences that raised concerns regarding the equity of higher education provision in Kenya. The first was that despite the growth in student numbers, the university had not adequately diversified its curricula or the composition of its student population. The university was seen as concentrating public resources on a few students. The curricula remained narrow and generally did not reflect the changing socioeconomic circumstances of Kenyan society. Public sentiments then were that such curricula were elitist, and gave advantage to regions and households that had benefited from the inequitable distribution of educational opportunities during the pre-independence days.

Second was the realisation that despite the role of the public university in skills and work force development, society was not benefiting equitably from the skills, as personnel were not distributed equitably. The university had concentrated in producing skills and developing a work force to replace departing white-collar expatriates, to the detriment of rural agriculture and small-scale industry. The majority of rural farmers, small-scale traders and pastoralists in ASAL areas were not accessing qualified work force skills from higher education in order to improve their productive capacity. Most of the graduates from universities were concentrated in urban areas and in the manufacturing sector in an economy that heavily relied on rural agriculture. There was therefore need to expand higher education towards meeting the development needs of rural communities.

In 1981, and given the above concerns, the government of Kenya appointed a presidential working party to study and recommend modalities of expanding higher education through the establishment of a second university. The significance of the recommendations of the working party for this study is in terms of the pace they set in legalising the development of private higher education in the country (Republic of Kenya 1981) Besides recommending the establishment of a second public university in a rural setting, three other recommendations supported higher education expansion through private resources. First, the working party noted the strain on existing public resources, and recommended that any future expansion had to match student enrolment with the resources available. The idea was to ensure that quality and relevance in university teaching, research and scholarship were maintained and enhanced. To this end, the working party proposed, and it was the first time such a proposal was officially made, that consideration be given to the development of good 'Harambee' as well as private university institutions. Such institutions would offer increased opportunities for local university education and training. However, their establishment was to be carefully controlled and guided to enhance the proper development and maintenance of acceptable university standards of teaching and research.

Second, it was proposed that public universities be encouraged to admit more students who were qualified on condition that they paid tuition fees, instead of depending on government grants. The prevailing situation, and one that obtained up to the mid-1990s, was that admission to public higher education institutions was pegged to the government's financial ability to meet students' tuition and non-tuition expenses, and the available bed space at the institutions. This meant that qualified candidates could miss admission if financial resources from the government were inadequate. Such a policy did not take into consideration the fact that some families were able to meet their children's higher education expenses, and treated all students the same regardless of socioeconomic background. The admission policies continued to exacerbate inequitable access to higher education in the country. Although the government continued to capitalise the university loan scheme as a revolving fund, recovery of the monies from past loans was too inefficient to benefit the growing number of students seeking admission, as early envisaged. For example, by 1988, the government had disbursed a total of Ksh 1,273,814,580 to 93,899 university students. However, only 2,844 past students were repaying their loans. The proposal for the semi-privatisation of public higher education by admitting qualified students who would be able to finance their studies was therefore timely. This has become a prevalent mode of privatisation of higher education in Kenya.

Third, the working party made a proposal for the establishment of a council for higher education. The council once established would ensure that the establishment of private universities was related to national planning. Such a body was subsequently established in 1985 by an Act of Parliament as the Commission for Higher Education (CHE).

Fourth, a proposal was made to the effect that the envisaged second university, and by extension future developments in higher education, had to have a different thrust and a change in emphasis. Such institutions were to be based in the rural areas, and were to emphasise science and technology courses that fused academic programmes with the realities of Kenya's social and cultural life. The second public university that was established because of this recommendation lived up to these criteria. It was established in a rural setting, in the western part of the country. The university also focussed more on establishing academic programmes in technological fields in agriculture, science, forestry medicine and veterinary medicine. These were the areas in which that the country required high-level skills, in terms of its development objectives. Therefore, if the establishment of private higher education institutions were a true response to the country's development needs, it is important to analyse the extent to which they have actually addressed such a demand. It is also important to define the market for higher education within this context, and not only in terms of skills that provide students with job opportunities and monetary rewards, and therefore generate a sense of profit to both the employer and the employee in the short term. The untapped potential in terms of the demand for skills to improve the production capacity of Kenya's rural areas and to meet the people's expectations is in a sense a 'market' that higher education and training should respond to. The extent to which private higher education has addressed this challenge will be discussed later in this study.

The 1990s: The 'take off' stage of private higher education in Kenya

The conditions for the development of private higher education in Kenya evolved in the late-1970s and in the 1980s. However, it was in the 1990s that private higher education approached the take off threshold in the country. Various conditions facilitated this take off.

First, as already indicated, the Commission for Higher Education (CHE) had been created in 1985. Part of the responsibilities of the Commission was to co-ordinate post-secondary education and training for the purpose of higher education and university admissions. This responsibility entailed that the CHE, among other things, set standards and bestowed recognition of qualifications for both public and private higher education institutions. Public universities however had a vice-chancellors' committee that operated as the Joint Admissions Board (JAB) for the purpose of regulating admissions. This committee still exists and apportions the admission of regular students among public universities. Given the entrenched political influence of the vice-chancellors, and the manner of their appointment to office, they have never allowed the CHE to superintend the operations of public universities. This conflict continues to limit the role of the CHE to accrediting and supervising private universities. The situation helped facilitate the accreditation of private universities whose applications had for long been pending. The fact that a body that had been legally mandated by the public through parliament was the one to accredit private universities gave them a stamp of approval in the eyes of the public. This helped to 'market' their image as credible institutions that were an acceptable alternative to public universities. Before the establishment of CHE, there were no specific procedures for the development of private higher education in Kenya. Previously, an application for registration to the permanent secretary in the Ministry of Education was all that was required. There were no formal criteria to judge the quality of standards in the private institutions. By 1985, eleven institutions had been granted letters of registration and operated as universities.

Second was a combination of factors that revolved around the financial inability of the government to continue subsidising an ever-expanding public higher education system. From 1985, Kenya started implementing structural adjustment programmes (SAPS), as part of reform initiatives driven by the World Bank and bilateral donors. The programmes required among other things (see Williamson 1999), reforms in the education sector, especially a reduction of government subsidies to university education. Other specific conditions included a redirection of public expenditure towards fields offering high economic returns and the potential to improve income distribution such as primary health care, primary education and infrastructure. Privatisation and liberalisation of social service provision were also included. These reforms were meant to facilitate a transition from state to market planning. Since public higher education previously benefited from the statist approach, any reforms towards privatisation or liberalising its provision were to shake the foundations on which it had always stood. Privatisation and liberalisation of higher education in Kenya was therefore foremost a consequence of these donor conditions, especially as they were tied to Kenya receiving certain aid packages.

Kenya did not implement the above conditions immediately, especially those that demanded reforms in the financing of higher education. Instead, the government continued expanding higher education without commensurate resources. The expansion that took place in public higher education from 1985 to 1990, when Kenya was supposed to have been privatising, explains the fanfare with which private universities were embraced in the 1990s. Mixed with an act of defiance to donors and the search for political popular support, the Kenyan political leadership went about transforming most diploma-level non-university institutions to universities. This was accompanied by political declarations from the political leadership to university authorities to relax the academic criteria for admission to take in more students. For example, in the 1987–1988 academic year, the government made a policy decision to admit a double class of first years into the public universities (Wandiga 1997). This was made necessary in order to clear the backlog created from the closure of the universities due to the attempted coup in 1982. Besides, Kenya had changed its education system from 7-4-2-3 to 8-4-4. The first group of 8-4-4 students were expected to enter the university in 1990, together with the last group of students from the 7-4-2-3 'A' level system that was being phased out. Both the 1987–1988 and 19901–1991 double intakes were accompanied by the admission of more other students than was the case previously due to the relaxation of admission requirements. The 1987–1988 double intake alone increased student numbers in the public universities by 75.2 percent from 8,804 to 15,337 students.

The expansion did not take place in terms of student numbers alone. Upgrading some middle level colleges to university status also increased the number of public universities. In the 1983–1984 academic year, there were two public university institutions, namely Nairobi and Moi universities. Kenyatta University College, a constituent of the University of Nairobi, was upgraded to a fully-fledged university in 1985. Combined they had a student population of 5,174 students (Republic of Kenya 1991). In the 1986–1987 academic year a fifth university, the Jomo Kenyatta University College of Agriculture and Technology, was established. During the second double intake of the 1990–1991 academic year, a sixth university institution, Maseno, was established. These developments pushed student enrolment in public universities to 38,848 (Wandiga 1997).

The critical factor was that adequate resources to sustain quality did not mark the above expansion. On the contrary, financial resources from the government continued to decrease as expansion of the institutions was intensified. Gross government expenditure on university education, as a percentage distribution of the Ministry of Education, fell from 20.9 percent in the 1989–1990 academic year to 18.3 percent in the 1991–1992 academic year, to 17.2 percent in the 1993–1994 academic year (Wandiga 1997). The scenario undermined the quality of education and other services in the public universities. The ever-expanding public education created a rush for university education in Kenya. For students from high school who qualified but who did not receive admission to the public universities, the push for private provision locally became an alternative to the elusive overseas higher education. India, that was up to then the most open destination for Kenyan students, was suffering a negative press in Kenya that undermined the credibility of academic certificates from some Indian Universities. Some working Kenyans who had not had a chance for a university level education started looking for such chances to remain relevant and enhance chances of job mobility. At the public universities, overcrowding and lack of adequate teaching facilities occasioned frequent student riots and university closures. This dampened the image of public universities as cradles of quality learning. Students and their families resorted to private universities as alternatives. This factor alone pushed private universities to seek accreditation and to expand their facilities.

Even in the midst of the above scenarios, the government was not keen on privatising higher education entirely. This reluctance was perhaps dictated by political considerations rather a genuine desire to raise the efficiency of public higher education in Kenya. Therefore, in the face of increasing demand and dwindling resources for higher education, the government tried to search for alternatives to salvage public higher education. However, the ripple effects of any policy actions from the government not only provided a strong argument for liberalising higher education provision, but also actually created a demand for private higher education within the public psyche.

Faced with pressure to admit more students, with overcrowding in universities and a subsequent lowering in quality, the government requested an emergency loan of USD 600 million from the World Bank, under the education sector adjustment credit (EdSAC). The credit was targeted to improve access, quality, equity and management of public higher education (D'Souza 2001). The World Bank did not approve the whole amount requested, releasing only USD 60 million, and attached to the funds certain conditionalities. The government was asked to offer public higher education at market rates by introducing direct charges for tuition in public universities and reforming the student loan scheme to make recovery of loaned money efficient. Second and more critical, the number of students admitted to public universities was capped at 10,000 regardless of the total number of qualified applicants. This condition is still applied up to the present. The effect of this condition has been to create a ready market for private universities, as qualified students have taken private universities as a first choice alternative to public universities. The introduction of the reforms also led to very limited public resources at the universities, thus constraining their efforts at expansion.

The period of rapid expansion of public universities and the massification of student intake to the institutions therefore played a key role in the acceptance of private universities and the form into which they subsequently evolved. Parents and students who did not want to be associated with the academic rot that had engulfed public universities resorted to the few private universities that were already in existence. The internal trends towards the evolution of private universities were bolstered by the growing internationalisation of higher education, and the recognition in international policy environments of the private sector in the provision of elite higher education institutions. Within this context, the private universities that evolved in Kenya did not encompass the broad mandate of higher education as previously known. Rather they targeted an elite, defined in terms of both the socioeconomic background of students and the key markets that required their skills. It is within this context that CHE, created in 1985, and that hitherto had undertaken little activity as regards its mandate, accelerated the process of granting charters and letters of interim registration for private universities.

The World Bank conditionalities that limited the number of student admitted to public universities and introduced tuition fees, the haphazard expansion of public universities, and the ever-increasing demand for university education were a major impetus to the recognition and growth of private higher education. Henceforth, the government accepted and entrenched private universities as complementary to the provision of public higher education. By 1990, Kenya had eleven registered private universities. By 1994, three private universities; Baraton University, Catholic University and Daystar University had been accredited by CHE and given charters to award their own internationally recognised degrees. Besides, by 1994, the government had put in place mechanisms to strengthen the role of CHE to coordinate the growth of university level education. Table 2.0 summarises the state of the various private universities in Kenya by 2003.

Table 2.0: Number and status of private universities in Kenya, 2003

	Institution	Date Established CHE	Date Registered	Date accredited with CHE
1.	Nairobi International School of Theology	1981	1989	Not yet
2.	Nairobi Evangelical Graduate School of Theology	1983	1989	Not yet
3.	East African School of Theology	1979	1989	Not yet
4.	Pan-African Christian College	1978	1985	Not yet
5.	St Paul's Theological College	1980	1985	Not yet
6.	Scott Theological College	1986	1988	1997
7.	Kenya Highlands Bible College	1971	1989	Not yet
8.	Daystar University	1978	1989	1994
9.	African Nazarene University	1994	1994	2002
10.	Catholic University of East Africa (CUEA)	1984	1992	1994
11.	University of East Africa Baraton (UEAB)	1978	1991	1991
12.	United States International University (USIU)	1970	1989	1999
13.	Kabarak University	1998	2000	Not yet
14.	Kenya Methodist University	1997	1997	Not yet
15.	Kiriri Women's University of Science and Technology	2002	2002	Not yet
16.	Agha Khan University	2002	2002	Not yet
17.	Strathmore University	2002	2002	Not yet

Source: Private university statistics CHE: 2004

Table 2.0 summarises certain background characteristics on the status of private universities in Kenya. Such characteristics define the mission and objectives of the universities. To the extent that the private universities operate autonomously based on their missions, the associated characteristics influence the degree to which they respond to issues such as equity in their operations. For example, of the 17 Universities registered with the CHE by 2003, 15 of them were sponsored by religious organisations. Their missions and academic programmes also had a strong religious orientation. This fact alone, though not explicitly stated in the institutions' mission statements, could operate to exclude access of students from certain sections of society. Secondly it is evident that most of the private universities were established and registered between 1970 and 1989. All the seventeen Universities are also registered with CHE, a fact that demonstrates their desire for official recognition and acceptance.

The Kenya government has put in place policies to promote the growth of private universities while ensuring they offer quality programmes. From the 1997–2001 plan periods, the government took several policy decisions.

First, an act of parliament in 1995 established the Higher Education Loans Board (HELB). The board facilitates the financing of student tuition in an efficient market-driven manner. With the inauguration of the board, and subsequent policy developments, students in all higher education, institutions (both private and public) are eligible to apply and receive a tuition loan to finance their studies. The fact that even students in private higher education institutions qualify for financing from a publicly capitalised institution is a boost to the growth of private higher education. In the 2002–2003, academic year, 15 percent of students in private universities were getting tuition loans from HELB.

Second, the government through the Ministry of Education and CHE, in consultation with public and private higher education institutions, has implemented proposals to ease admission and entry of the students to the various institutions based on the students' choices. For example, reforms have been put in place to allow qualifying students to seek admission to colleges and universities of their choice. This was in view of past practices where qualifying students were restricted to take up places in public universities even when they were not placed in programmes of their choice. This practice had to be overtaken by the realisation that students pay equal tuition fees, and should be allowed to choose courses of their choice, and such choices be linked to prevailing market forces. A system of credit transfer and accreditation of middle higher education institutions is being worked out on a continuous basis. This policy reform indicated the extent to which the government appreciates the role private universities play in the provision of higher education. It will therefore be necessary for the private institutions to reciprocate by broadening their missions to include aspects that address wider social issues other than clinging to their narrow elitist character.

Third, and this is in regard to public universities, declining resources from the government for development forced administrators to start admitting students who qualify and who would pay tuition fees at determined market rates. This has marked the third phase in the evolution of private higher education in Kenya. Privately sponsored (popularly known as parallel degree students) are now a major component of the student population in public universities. According to the Government of Kenya *2003 Economic Survey*, the government sponsors only 55 percent of the total student enrolment in public universities (Republic of Kenya 2003). The remaining 45 percent are private and if added to those in private universities, then the percentage of students in private higher education would be slightly more than the public one. This fact alone means that the private universities and programmes can no longer remain elitist, but must integrate their missions and operations to the development needs of the country. The numbers of regular admissions from qualifying students to public universities continue to decline, as the parallel admission continue to increase in all public universities. The competition for students has been intensified between public universities and private universities and between public universities themselves in terms of entry of students to specific courses that are seen to be more 'marketable' (in terms of job placement and expected remuneration).

Table 2.1 below summarises the enrolment of students in selected private universities, between 1996–1997 and the 2002–2003 academic years. The period was when public universities faced a crisis of confidence from the public. Information in the table captures the pattern in the growth of students in private universities, and therefore a critical period in their evolution. This pattern does not show plummeting enrolments like those witnessed in public universities in the 1987–1988 and 1990–1991 academic years.

Table 2.1: Student enrolments in accredited private universities in Kenya 1996–1997 to 2002–2003 academic years

Institution	1996-7	1997-8	1998-9	1999-2000	2000-1	2001-02	2002-03
Daystar University	1,250	1,292	1,681	2,278	1,812	1,864	2,135
Baraton University	922	842	952	1,044	1,306	1,127	1,531
Catholic University	1,207	1,320	1,402	1,617	1,477	1,574	1,803
United States International University	1,753	1,808	1,901	1,960	2,311	2,544	3,106
Scott Theological College	78	82	96	103	93	102	105
Totals	5,210	5,344	6,032	7,002	6,999	7,211	8,680

Source: Kenya Statistical Abstracts 2004.

The figures from Table 2.1 show a gradual but steady increase of student enrolments in the various private universities. The highest growth was in the 1998–1999 and 1999–2000 academic years when the percentage increase of students was about 16 percent. The 2000–2001 and 2001–2002 academic years saw a slight increase of 3.02 percent, which again fluctuated to a high of 20.4 percent between the 2001–2002 and 2002–2003 academic years. Nevertheless, the real significance of this growth in terms of higher education expansion in Kenya, and equity should be understood against the context of what was happening in the public universities. This is important in drawing conclusions about the role of private higher education in expanding access and equity to higher education in comparison to public universities. Such a comparison can shed light on certain perceptions that have been held about private universities as critical alternatives to quality higher education. As has been indicated, legislation that governed the management of public universities together with donor conditionalities limited the leeway they enjoyed in admitting more students. However, the financial crunch occasioned by decreasing resources from the government forced public universities to start admitting private students at market tuition rates. This gave the students another alternative to higher education besides the purely private universities. The impact this has had in increasing access to university education in Kenya will be discussed later. It is however important at this point to provide a typology of what private higher education in Kenya consists.

A Typology of private universities and programmes in Kenya

Before profiling the four private universities that were covered in the study it is important that a typology of what represents private higher education in Kenya be made. Private higher education is not homogeneous. Institutions that offer private higher education are differentiated in terms of their missions, mandates and sources of finance. In Kenya, as elsewhere in the developing countries where private higher education is just emerging, these differences are premised on whether the institutions are offering their programmes to generate profit (commercial logic), or whether they are offering a service to recoup operational costs without realising profits. The typology of 'not for profit' and 'for profit' institutions therefore is fitting in categorising private higher education institutions in Kenya.

(a) 'Not for profit' religious institutions

Understanding the background to the growth of these institutions to university status was critical to this study. Seminal literature on private higher education in Africa identifies Kenya to have a larger sector of these types of institutions. Most of these institutions have been established by religious bodies that took the first initiatives to provide private higher education. The 'not for profit' institutions still account for the largest number of private universities in the country. However, as will be seen from the data presented elsewhere in this study, these institutions enrol a small number of students compared to the total number who qualify for university admissions annually in the country. The largeness of this sector is therefore more in terms of number of institutions rather than in terms of volume of students enrolled. As the background to the study shows, the push for the establishment and regulation of private higher education institutions was from the social demand for university education. Expansion of secondary and other post-secondary institutions in the country had created a clamour for university degree education that the public universities were not able to meet. One is therefore certain to measure the place of private higher education institutions in terms of the extent to which they have expanded to meet this demand.

In developed economies where higher education has almost actualised the social demand imperatives, growth in this sector tends towards institutional diversity and response to specific group and corporate interests. In developing countries, the logic would be first to actualise a high degree of mass higher education by opening access to individuals who qualify from all social groups as a way of addressing social equity issues. This point has to be made because there are views that private universities do not have to respond to social demand and expand as long as they respond to the academic needs of their clients. Clients in this case are defined based on the small number of students who afford tuition fees charged by the institutions.

The 'not for profit' private universities in Kenya account for twelve of the seventeen private universities. These institutions operate at different levels. Five of them have been chartered by CHE and can award their own degrees .These universities are: the University of East Africa, Baraton (UEAB),The Catholic University of East Africa (CUEA), Daystar University, Scott Theological College, and African Nazarene University. One university, The Kenya Methodist University, has a letter of interim authority to operate. This means the university can admit and teach degree level students as it continues to implement other proposals from CHE to qualify for a charter. These proposals include diversification of the curriculum and upgrading of facilities. The last category here are institutions registered as universities but not operating as such. Some of them however offer degree programmes on behalf of other institutions. This has made them institutions of choice for local and foreign universities keen to establish arrangements for twinning academic programmes. Institutions in this category are the East Africa School of Theology, The Nairobi Evangelical Graduate School of Theology, the Nairobi International School of Theology, Pan African Christian College, Kenya Highlands Bible College, and St Paul's United Theological College.

All the 'not for profit' institutions base their curricula on some evangelical Christian beliefs and teachings. Besides the CUEA, UEAB, African Nazarene University and the Kenya Methodist University that offer both religious and secular curricula, the rest of the institutions in this category offer purely religious syllabi for those of their followers who want to join the ministry as preachers. Despite their high number therefore, most of these institutions target a few evangelical followers as their students. Over 90 percent of students enrolled in the 'not for profit' institutions are concentrated in four of the institutions that offer secular instruction. The growth of private higher education cannot be judged in terms of the number of institutions, but rather the number of students that are admitted and graduate from the institutions. On this score the 'not for profit' institutions give a false impression of a robust expanding private higher education sector in Kenya when the reality on the ground presents a different picture. Hence, in Kenya, religious private higher education institutions represent a higher share of higher education institutions, but a hold a small percentage of enrolments. As we shall show elsewhere in this study, USIU a secular for profit university, enrols more students and offers a wider curricula diversity than either UEAB or Daystar University, although the religious institutions were chartered earlier than USIU.

A more important issue that needs analysis is related to the higher number of religious-based institutions that account for this sector. All the institutions in this category were operating in Kenya a considerable time before higher education provision was liberalised. The Kenya capital, Nairobi, has served as Africa's ecumenical, missionary and para-church ministries centre for a long time (Carpenter 2003). For this reason, Nairobi hosts a large number of highly educated evangelical leaders, besides being home to a variety of Bible schools and Christian institutions. These leaders and institutions have been instrumental in transforming the nature of higher education provision from the private sector. The history of some of the institutions, such as Scott Theological College, dates back to the colonial period. The College was established by the African Inland Church to cater for the missionary needs of the time. Others, such as Daystar Communications, later Daystar University, were a post-independence development that expanded to serve the evangelical needs of some Christian churches. In addition, most Christian organisations used Kenya as a hub for their missionary work in East and Central Africa. The Catholics and Seventh Day Adventists who came to found CUEA and UEAB are a case in point. The attraction for establishing working bases from Kenya may have been motivated by the relative peace and robust economy that Kenya experienced in much of the 1970s and 1980s. The same logic may have influenced the expansion of Daystar communications from its base in Zimbabwe. These internal and accidental confluences led the Christian-based institutions to enjoy a numerical lead in the provision of private higher education in Kenya.

The numerical lead of the Christian churches however explains one part of the developments. The other part can be attributed to growth and change in the manner of operation of the evangelical churches worldwide. Joel Carpenter (2003), in an illuminating seminal essay, has characterised this process as the evangelical change of mission from producing Christian workers to producing Christian citizens. He attributes the growth of evangelical universities to a worldwide attempt by Christianity to confront the political and economic forces of globalisation with forms of Christian teaching that offer hope to the poor through higher education. In a sense, evangelical universities represent a religious response to certain exclusion tendencies of globalisation. Three important trends have marked out these developments.

First has been a new spirit of mission and agenda setting from Christian professionals and intellectuals who are lay persons unlike the clerics of the past. These new leadership is adept at finance and fundraising for the new evangelical universities. Second has been the rise of new players in global Christian mission work. These new players have taken the face of multinational Christian agencies, to use Carpenter's (2003: 62), phrase. The Christian multinational agencies parallel the economic and political multinational. These Christian multinationals have largely been responsible for financing the establishment of private universities. Lastly, the new evangelical universities emphasise the spirit of enterprise. This is not new in Christian thought. The Protestant Ethic was part of the rise of capitalism. What is important here is to show how the spirit of enterprise has coupled with the intellectual leadership of the evangelical churches to venture into private higher education provision. Again, this is not just a beginning of church involvement in higher education. The beginning of higher education from the medieval period was a missionary and church enterprise. What is new is that church established universities are spreading from their traditional citadels in the western world to Africa. This movement represents among others the concentration of new evangelical Christian followers in Africa. It also represents a departure from traditional Christian teaching of the afterlife to modern evangelical perceptions of Christian life.

Lastly is the issue of the extent to which the 'not for profit' evangelical universities are actually not for profit. Varghese (2004: 8) has characterised the not for profit institutions as those that are owned and operated by trusts (see also Levy 2003: 11-12). The institutions rely heavily on endowments, on fees collected from students and on support from religious agencies. These are contrasted with for-profit institutions that operate to produce profit. They rely on student fees as a major source of financing, offer courses on market-friendly subject areas and are at times affiliated to universities abroad. In many respects, the 'not for profit' private universities in Kenya fit into the category of for profit institutions, according to Varghese's conceptualisation. One would expect that since they are not for profit and since they receive assistance and endowments from elsewhere, their tuition fees could be lower than that charged by the for profit institutions. However, this study established that tuition expenses were almost at par in all the private universities.

The average annual fees charged for example by USIU, a private for profit institution at the time of this study were US$ 2,682 for arts-based courses and US$2,875 for science-based courses. These compared with annual tuition fees of US$1,843 (CUEA), US$2,893 (UEAB), and 2,453 (Daystar) for arts courses and US$ 2,160 (CUEA), 2,893 (UEAB), and 2,453 (Daystar) for science courses respectively. Of course, USIU also had other charges that considerably added to the annual fees charged by between US$1500–2000. Both 'for profit' and the 'not for profit' institutions were therefore engaged in market-like behaviour in terms of pricing their courses. The differences in the tuition fees charged are too small really to reflect the 'not for profit' tag of the religiously inclined private universities.

Another aspect related to the issue of fees are various other charges levied on students at the private universities. These charges were grouped into optional and non-optional. The non- optional charges are those that a student has to pay along with tuition fees to access certain university services. The optional charges are left at the discretion of the student but non-payment means exclusion from accessing certain services. At UEAB, the non-optional expenses such as library, equipment, room and food, medical and caution fees totalled Kenyan shillings 94,300 (US$ 1257). This made total annual charges go up to Kenyan shillings 236,860 (US$ 3158). The cumulative charges of UEAB were in this respect higher compared to USIU. Hence, the religious private universities are legally registered as 'not for profit' institutions but operationally they charge tuition fees and other levies that are at par and sometimes beyond what the 'for profit' institutions charge. This is the more interesting given that their legal status allows the institutions to procure certain services and commodities tax- free.

The second issue related to the 'not for profit' status relates to the curricula. Most of the courses offered in the not for profit institutions are those that have been considered market-friendly. In Varghese's conceptualisation, they mark a for-profit oriented institution. These are vocational courses in Business Studies and Administration and Computer, information technology and applied sciences. All the religious 'not for profit' institutions in Kenya offer these programmes at certificate, diploma and degree levels. There are also professional areas such as continuing teacher education that have a high applicant rate in both private and public universities. Of course, religious criteria in admission and teaching are infused in the admission and curricular criteria of the institutions. However, largely their curricula responds to the market and they peg admission on ability to pay tuition fees over anything else. These issues continue to raise doubts on the 'not for profit' status of these institutions. It may be that more studies on the conceptual categorisation of private higher education institutions versus the flow of resources to these institutions are needed. Keeping the 'not for profit' tag while charging tuition fees, offering curricula and restricting student admission on their ability to pay erodes the existence of a large sector of not for profit private higher education institutions in Kenya.

(b) *The for profit secular institutions and programmes*

Three categories of institutions comprise the for profit private sector of higher education in Kenya. First are the established private universities. At the time of this study, five such universities were operational. These were USIU, the single largest secular private university both in terms of physical facilities and of student numbers. USIU was chartered by CHE in 1999, although it had been in Kenya on a small scale from the earlier 1970s. The other universities in this category are Kabarak University, Agha Khan University, Strathmore University and Kiriri Women's University of Science and Technology. These four universities had not been accredited by the time of the study. Their operations are limited to the provisions of the letter of Interim Authority. The letter issued by CHE allows the institutions to operate as universities as they upgrade their facilities in preparation for inspection for purposes of receiving accreditation. They are also small scale in terms of their curricula and student numbers. Kabarak and Kiriri Women's University have been set up by individual proprietors while Strathmore and Agha Khan belong to groups with business acumen. Though secular, Kabarak, Strathmore and Agha Khan have been sponsored by individuals and groups with strong religious affiliations. Strathmore has a strong affiliation to the Catholic Church, Agha Khan to the Ismail Muslims, and the sponsor of Kabarak, former President Moi, to the African Inland Church.

Despite its legal status as a private for profit secular university, the mission statement of Kabarak invokes Christian principles as the basis of its functional foundations. Strathmore University despite its link to the Catholic Church has a strong secular and for profit orientation in its operations. The University is part of the Global Business School Network (GBSN), an initiative of the International Finance Corporation (IFC), a private sector arm of the World Bank. The mission of the university is also framed in secular terms: to provide quality business and information technology education in an environment that promotes an entrepreneurial mindset and ethical practices.

The Agha Khan and Kiriri Women's Universities are also unique in some respects. Agha Khan's curricula tend towards nursing and medical courses. These courses have been avoided by the other private universities, as they require heavy capital investments. This is one area where there is a national and regional demand for a professional workforce. Kiriri, on the other hand, has focussed not only on women but also on areas from which women have been traditionally excluded. The two universities seem to have defined the market not in terms of training in short-term vocational skills, as the other private universities have done. Their focus is on the long-term professional requirements of the global market. Indeed skills, especially in medicine and nursing, are in high demand globally and Agha Khan seems to have been positioned to address this demand in the long-term.

The second category of the private for profit higher education provision comprises private programmes offered at public universities. These programmes are considered for profit since commercial and market-like behaviour governs the admission of students and the operation of the programmes. Lecturers who teach these students receive extra payment besides their salaries. Much of the revenue is of course used to subsidise university operations and development. However, the income is shared across all the university personnel as trading partners share profits. All public universities in Kenya admit students who pay full tuition fees and their accommodation and subsistence expenses are not subsidised either by the universities or the government. These admissions are besides the regular students whose tuition and accommodation expenses are subsidised.

The full tuition-paying students are referred to variously as 'privately sponsored', 'parallel degree', 'continuing education' or 'module two students'. The various terms designate the sources of tuition fees for the students, the nature of academic programmes into which they are admitted, the manner of teaching and of evaluation, or both. Their sources of finance are private, meaning individual savings or from family and parents. They are referred to as parallel because in some instances their academic programmes are conducted separately from those of regular students although course content is the same. Coverage may however vary depending on the amount of hours covered, especially for evening and weekend classes and those conducted when regular students are on three-month vacations. The 'continuing' label refers to working students who are pursuing studies for purposes of job mobility. These students are referred in this study as private students. The motivation to launch these programmes by public universities was to generate extra income. With decreasing government financial support, the university authorities resorted to these programmes. The income generated is supposed to be used to improve the quality of teaching and learning facilities to benefit the whole student community. The efficiency with which the extra revenues are generated and used to improve the quality of academic programmes in public universities is important in analysing the implications of privatising public universities.

In line with the commercial culture of private higher education, some universities have formed corporate companies and corporate-like entities to manage the financial aspects of the programmes and to advise on business plans institutions. The University of Nairobi, for example, formed the University of Nairobi enterprise services (UNES). UNES functions like a corporate entity within the university, and the management and functional aspects of the company are guided by the state corporations Act. Other public universities have separate income-generating directorates. Through such directorates, Jomo Kenyatta University of Science and Technology collaborates with public and private middle level colleges to offer continuing education programmes at venues convenient to students. All public universities have set up various mechanisms to admit extra students who pay fees at market rates as with private universities in order to generate operational resources. To push more students to take up the private alternative, public universities have consistently capped their regular admissions to 10,000 students. Admission of regular students to competitive professional courses such as law, medicine, engineering, computer science and science teacher education is also limited to take in more fee-paying students. The admission of private students to public universities, the commercialisation of academic programmes and the corporate manner in which the programmes are managed constitute the privatisation of public universities in Kenya.

The introduction of private degree students in public universities has greatly stalled the growth of purely private universities. Data for this study show that enrolments in private universities went up during academic years when public universities had not started the private programmes. For example during the academic year 1995–1996, enrolments in public universities declined by 10.3 percent. In the 1996–1997 academic year, the decline was in the range of six percent (Republic of Kenya, Statistical Abstracts 2003). This saw an increase of 2.7 percent in the five key private universities that constitute over 90 percent of enrolments in private universities. During the 1998–1999 academic year when enrolment in public Universities declined by about seven percent, growth in the private universities within the same period almost doubled to 16 percent. However, during the 2001–2002 academic year when public universities increased enrolment by 24.5 percent, those in private universities increased only by 3.02 percent. The 2000–2001 academic year saw public universities intensify admission of private students for various degree and diploma courses.

Two conclusions can be made here. One, privatisation of higher education within public universities has led to a near stagnation of enrolments in private universities.

Two, private universities were an alternative when public universities had not opened up to private students. This meant they were the only choice available locally. Without competition, it is hard to conclude therefore that they constituted a better choice. It is also not wise to conclude that the quality of academic programmes in private universities was higher because more students had opted for them. As has been argued, this happened during a period when public universities were suffering a credibility crisis. The scenario in most of Africa in the 1980s and 1990s was that private provision of services was preached as an alternative to poor quality services that were offered in government-managed facilities. These perceptions were based on the key assumptions of the neo-liberal reforms that almost demonised public service provision as inefficient in comparison with private provision. Any institution that provided education and other social services privately was taken in the public psyche to mean efficiency and better quality. However, as public service reforms in Africa now attest, the privatisation drive went to 'fundamentalist' levels and did not necessarily lead to quality services. This explains the high number of students opting for private programmes in public universities and the near stagnation of enrolments in purely private universities in Kenya. This could also be attributed to the diversity of academic programmes that public universities offered in comparison with the purely private universities. These considerations usually underlie students' choice of institutions.

The third institution in the for profit category is the African virtual university (AVU). The AVU, headquartered in Nairobi, utilises satellite technology and e-learning techniques to deliver academic programmes. It offers undergraduate and postgraduate programmes based on prioritised needs of students. The areas that have been targeted are those considered critical for economic development. Like its other private counterparts, AVU has focussed on computer science, computer engineering, electrical and mechanical engineering, public health, teacher training, business administration and commerce. All the public universities in Kenya act as AVU teaching centres. The academic programmes that AVU uses have been developed and transmitted by universities in America and Europe. These universities are the Massachusetts Institute of Technology (USA), Carleton University (Canada), Université Laval (Canada), New Jersey Institute of Technology, (USA), Indiana Institute of Technology (USA), Royal Melbourne Institute of Technology (Australia), and Curtin University (Australia). In the long term, the mission of AVU is to develop the capacity of African academics in open learning, distance education and e-learning. While the learning techniques sound sophisticated and the revolutionary potential attractive, this study was not able to access information on programme costs and the number of students enrolled from Kenya. It is however instructive that virtual learning techniques aim to cut costs of face-to-face instruction and in Africa represent the face of the global multinational university. The partners of AVU include organisations such as the European Union and the World Bank, bilateral donors such as DfID, and national governments in Africa.

The foregoing provides a summary of how expansive privatising and private higher education is in Kenya. What is tricky is to draw a line between for-profit and the not-for-profit institutions. This is because all the institutions charge almost the same amount of fees, engage in commercial and market-like behaviour, and on the basis of their missions, their clients are restricted in the main to the limited number of students who can afford tuition and other related costs. In the following section, the profiles of the four private universities that were covered by the study are discussed. This is necessary to capture the institutional orientations and mission statements of the various institutions to determine the extent of inclusion or exclusion of certain groups of students. This information has been used to draw conclusions on the extent to which the operations of the institutions address equity issues.

Profiles of the four private universities in the study

(a) The United States International University for Africa (USIU)

The history of USIU in Kenya dates back to 1969 when it moved its international presence to Nairobi from San Diego in the USA. During the same year, it was granted a presidential charter by Kenya's first president to operate in Kenya as a university institution. This made USIU the first and only secular private university in East Africa. The overriding philosophy of USIU, which could be traced to its founder Dr William Rust, was to 'bring together people of the world based on the belief that neither individuals nor nations can flourish in isolation'. The university therefore sought to create global understanding and cooperation through education. The university started operations in 1970 with five American students. Initially the students could start with a two-year programme in Kenya and proceed to San Diego to complete their studies there. By 1979, all programmes could be completed from the Nairobi campus and a Master's degree had been added to its academic offerings. USIU in this respect became the pioneer private secular university in the East African region.

The pioneer status gave the university an earlier advantage in responding to the rising demand for higher education in the country. USIU developed along with the increase in the number of students looking for university places and the decline in the public university sector. These factors meant USIU had to target an already identified clientele that had been 'captured' for the institution by circumstances. In 1989, the institution applied for a charter from CHE. The charter was awarded on 10 December 1999. USIU is also accredited by the Western association of schools and colleges (WASC) from the USA. This double accreditation has significantly raised the stature of the university as regards the quality of its programmes. USIU became the fifth private university to be accredited as such in Kenya. What is curious here is that despite the institution's earlier entry to provide secular private higher education, the other religious leaning institutions were given charters earlier. The explanation for this anomaly lay in the political climate in which CHE was then operating. The political leadership may have had a soft attitude towards religious leaning institutions. The President of the Republic confessed Christianity. He later established a private secular university, Kabarak, whose mission and philosophy are based on Christian teachings. However, more importantly was the political hostility towards privatisation and liberalisation at the time. Since reforms in these areas were packaged together with demands for political reforms, the political leadership viewed any private initiative as part of a challenge to its hegemony. USIU may have suffered this misplaced aggression as its religiously inclined competitors enjoyed more favourable treatment.

The goals of the university according to its mission statements are 'to provide a diverse community of learners with high quality, broad-based educational programmes that promote inquiry, masterly and application of knowledge through concepts and skills while fostering ethical leadership and responsible service to Kenya Africa and the challenging global community'. The mission statement guides the university in its admission policies and its conduct of academic programmes. The specific objectives that the university pursues, based on information summarised from the calendar, are:

- Supplying the work force to meet national requirements;
- Contributing to the knowledge and information needed for economic development;
- Increasing the enrolment of foreign students, hence gaining from foreign human and financial capital;
- Strengthening leadership qualities through education and training programmes;
- Ensuring that ethical and moral attributes and attitudes built into its programmes are applicable to the Kenyan workplace; and
- Strengthening the cultural base through study, research and diversity in student enrolments.

At the time of this study, USIU had an enrolment of 3,106 students, 53 percent of whom were female. The university continues to have the highest enrolment among the private universities. The success of the university in terms of enrolments and the projection of its image lies in a balanced articulation of the university's commercial objectives and the academic aspirations of its students. Three factors are frequently cited by students and staff as influencing their decision to study and work at USIU: (i) The international orientation of the staff, students and curricula combined. Sixteen percent of the faculty at USIU at the time of this study was non-Kenyan. To the students this means valued exposure to establish connections and enhance chances of working outside Kenya after graduation. To the faculty, the USIU connections have made it easier for them to pursue higher academic training in American universities. For both students and faculty these options are tempting at a time when getting a visa to the USA, even for studies, may be elusive. (ii) The dual accreditation of the university has attracted both Kenyan and foreign students. The university has used this effectively to market its programmes as of high quality and accepted worldwide. This captures the international students and Kenyan students who have aspirations of seeking employment outside Kenya. (iii) The re-branding of academic programmes to suit prevailing market demands. The university, for example offers an undergraduate and postgraduate degree in International Business Administration that is popular to both working and non-working students. It also forges links with major multinational companies and agencies where it places students for internships. Learning through internship is a course requirement at USIU and, unlike in the other universities where students look for placements on their own, USIU does this for its students and factors performance during internship into a student's graduation grades.

The university has also expanded its programmes from what it was offering ten years ago. Like all other private and public universities in Kenya USIU's academic programmes target both degree and non-degree students. This trend has been one development of private higher education where the functions of middle level vocational colleges are taken up by universities. Private and public universities in Kenya offer vocational and academic professional training. The level of training also ranges from certificate to postgraduate qualifications. This represents a departure from the pre-privatisation period when universities focussed on degree-level professional academic programmes. The vocational training was the mandate of the non-university sector of higher education institutions. The following degree programmes are offered at USIU:

- Undergraduate and postgraduate degrees in Business Administration;
- Undergraduate and postgraduate degrees in International Business Administration;
- Bachelor of Arts and Master of Arts in International Relations and Psychology;
- Bachelor of Arts in Journalism;
- Masters of Arts in Counselling Psychology;
- Masters of Science in Management and Organisational Development;
- Bachelor in Hotel and Restaurant Management;
- Bachelor of Science in Information Systems and Technology;
- Bachelor of Science in Tourism Management.

(b) The University of Eastern Africa – Baraton (UEAB)

The UEAB started in Kenya in 1978 when the Board of the Afro-Mid East division of the Seventh Day Adventists applied to the government to start a university. This was a logical progression of the church's involvement in educational provision that had started decades earlier. From 1903, the Seventh Day Adventist church had been established in Tanzania. From there, it spread to Uganda and Kenya and by the time the East African countries were gaining independence, the church was actively involved in setting up schools and colleges in the region. One challenge the church had to address was how to link its Christian beliefs to the secular education provided by the schools and colleges it had established in East Africa. This challenge led the church to limit recruitment of students and staff to those who shared in the beliefs and faith of the church. The institutionalisation of church practices required training institutions for its various cadres of workers. Before the establishment of UEAB, the church had to send its personnel to the Middle East College in Beirut, Lebanon for such training. The growth of the church faithful and non-university institutions made local training in East Africa necessary and urgent.

The need for institutionalising degree level education and training for the church's workforce was therefore the driving force for the establishment of UEAB. The urgency in meeting the growing social demand for higher education in Kenya and the East African region was not part of its initial mission. The government however supported the establishment of the university through the allocation of 339 acres of land of what was then a public animal husbandry research institute in Nandi district. This government support, as noted when discussing the case of USIU has not been forthcoming to private secular universities. (Not that the government has similarly supported all private religious leaning universities). However, at the period of their inception, faith-based institutions did not experience much trouble from government bureaucracy compared to those that the secular universities had to surmount. For example, the government allocated public land to UEAB, USIU, which had an earlier presence in the country, had to buy land for its development and expansion. The UEAB, with financial and personnel support from the SDA church, admitted the first group of students in January 1980. Tuition fees from students and philanthropic contributions supplement these funds. The student enrolment at the university stood at 1,531 at the time of the study. The university also is the largest Seventh Day Adventist institution on the continent of Africa.

The university, like USIU, also boasts of a double accreditation. First, it is accredited by the Association of Seventh Day Adventist Schools, Colleges and Universities. Second, it was given a charter by the government of Kenya on 28 March 1991. UEAB was actually the first private institution to be accredited by CHE to operate as an autonomous private university.

The mission of the UEAB is stated in its brochure as the 'provision and advancement of a holistic Christian quality education to equip learners with the necessary skills for service for God and the humanity'. The academic programmes of the institution and the culture of the university are based on this mission. This mission is anchored in the following two pillars of the Adventist philosophy. First, its philosophy on the nature of society is explicitly religious. The university sees the tensions and problems in contemporary society as a results of man's alienation from God. Therefore, the restoration of man's relationship to God is the foundation for healing what is broken in society. Second, it views all true knowledge as having its source in God. This knowledge is made available to people through programmes for the general public, as well as developing educated citizens who can meet the needs of the community and the Seventh Day Adventist church.

Based on the foregoing, the educational objectives of the university embody the following;

- The provision of balanced educational programmes that give each student the opportunity to develop socially;
- Encouraging students to understand appreciate and adopt a Christian lifestyle and value system;
- Helping students to strive for mental excellence;
- Assisting students to achieve and maintain physical health;
- Preparing students to become useful members of society;
- Preparing students for active service and a role in the mission of the Seventh Day Adventist church; and
- Providing adequate facilities and infrastructure for a high quality education.

The strict religious mission of the university has meant that it is accessible to students and faculty who profess the Adventist faith. Non-Adventist students and faculty, who agree to live according to Adventist lifestyles, are however considered for admission and employment. As the university states in its admission policy document, 'admission to the university is considered a privilege not a right'. The admission of non-Adventist students has however caused strains in the university. Even Adventist students' occasionally rebel against some of the strict Adventist ethos. The perception of students at UEAB was that the university does not have an enriching environment for secular education. The students pointed to daily worship and strict observance of the Sabbath as some of the issues that were not germane to pursuing a secular education. Observance of the Sabbath entails not listening to secular music and radio programmes, and not participating in sport functions and secular games. Avoiding reading secular materials and enforcement of Adventist morality in areas of eating and dress are also part of Sabbath observance. Importantly, Adventist teaching does not advocate affirmative action as it holds that 'all human beings to be equal without regard to race, gender, ethnicity and social statuses'. The desire to enforce Adventist teaching as part of a secular education has kept student numbers at UEAB small compared to the demand for higher education within East Africa. The university also admits international students. The focus on a target group of students and the admission of international students limits the impact of the university in addressing the social demand for higher education in Kenya.

The academic programmes of the university have expanded from what they were in the beginning. The various courses embody at least one facet of the university's mission statement. It is also important to note that UEAB provides academic programmes that are science-oriented. The academic programmes are organised into five schools, as follows:

- The School of Business, with Departments of Accounting, Management, Marketing, and Information Systems and Computing.
- The School of Education with Departments of Curriculum and Teaching and Guidance and Counselling.
- The School of Humanities and Social Sciences with Departments of History and Geography, Language and Literature, Theology and Religious Studies, Music.

- The School of Science and Technology, with Departments of Agriculture, Biological Sciences, Family and Consumer Sciences, Physical Sciences and Mathematics, Nursing, and Technology.
- The School of Public Health, offering a Masters in Public Health in collaboration with Loma Linda University.

(c) Daystar University

Daystar University, located in Nairobi, is non-denominational, and is the largest liberal arts college in Africa. Its origin dates back to 1967, when Dr Donald K. Smith, an American missionary, and S. E. M. Pheko founded Daystar Communications in Bulawayo, Zimbabwe, to evaluate various media used in communicating the message of Christ, to analyse the target audience of such messages, and to design and develop more effective communication strategies. In 1971, Daystar began short-term training programmes to assist church leaders in developing cross-cultural communication strategies. In 1976 it launched a two-year diploma programme; in 1978, a Master of Arts degree (in cooperation with Wheaton College, USA); and in 1984, a Bachelor of Arts degree (in cooperation with Messiah College, USA). In 1973, Daystar Communications was relocated to Nairobi and was registered as a non-profit company. Initially the College continued to offer undergraduate and graduate degrees, accredited by Messiah and Wheaton Colleges. In September 1994, Daystar was awarded a charter by the Kenyan government to become a fully-fledged university.

The mission of Daystar University is two-fold. First, it is to help church and missionary organisations to increase their effectiveness in communicating Christ to the culturally diverse societies of Africa. Second, it is to provide a university level educational centre where Christians throughout Africa can earn accredited degrees and be equipped as men and women of integrity (http://www.daystarus.org/mission.htm). The university is currently the only accredited evangelical Christian liberal arts college in all of black English-speaking Africa. Daystar also has double accreditation. Besides that from the Kenyan government, the university is accredited by the Christian College Consortium based in the USA. The university also admits international students. The student enrolment of Daystar stood at about 2,135 in 2003.

The revenue for running the university is derived from student tuition fees and contributions from sponsors. In this regard, the university gets support from Daystar, US, Daystar Canada, and affiliates within Africa. The University also prices its academic programmes at market rates and compares them to what other universities in North America and Europe charge. The academic programmes of the university reflect its mission and the diversity of students.

The courses offered at the university are:

- Bachelor of Arts in Bible and Religious Studies, Communication, Community Development, English, Music and Psychology.
- Bachelor of Commerce degree in Accounting, Business Administration and Management, Economics, Marketing.

- Bachelor of Education degree in Accounting, Bible and Religious Studies, Business Administration and Management, Economics and English, Marketing, and Music.
- Bachelor of Science degree in Computer Science, Economics.
- Masters of Arts degree in Christian Ministry Communication.
- A two-year diploma in Communication Arts, Christian Ministries and Counselling, Christian Ministries and Missions, Christian Music communication, Management and Development, Research and Consultation.

(d) Catholic University of Eastern Africa (CUEA)

The CUEA started as a graduate school of theology known as the Catholic Higher Institute of Eastern Africa (CHIEA), in 1984. The Institute was founded by the Regional Ecclesiastical authority known as the Association of Member Episcopal Conferences of Eastern Africa (AMECEA). The membership of the regional organisation comprises Eritrea, Ethiopia, Kenya, Malawi, Sudan, Tanzania, Uganda and Zambia. The impetus was the desire by Roman Catholic Bishops within the East African region for a Catholic University that would meet academic requirements and project an African view of the world. In August 1985, Pope John Paul II formally opened the institute. The graduate school of theology then started negotiations with the CHE in Kenya towards the establishment of the CUEA. In 1989, the institute obtained the 'letter of interim authority' as the first step towards its establishment as a private university. In 1992, the university was accredited and granted a charter.

The philosophy and vision of the university revolves around the desire to promote a universal Christian view and the pursuit of truth through consecration. This philosophy is articulated through the Catholic view of higher education. This teaching emphasises the free search for the whole truth about Nature, Humanity and God. According to this philosophy, higher education is pursued as an instrument of liberation and transformation and as an academic agent for creating knowledge and producing competent graduate leaders of the church.

The university offers certificate, diploma, undergraduate and post graduate programmes. The programmes are offered in five faculties. These are the faculties of Theology, Arts and Social Sciences, Science, Commerce, and Education. Finally, the University established an office to coordinate research and publications. This was a key difference from the other private universities, which focussed more on teaching and Christian education.

Private students and programmes at public universities

This section briefly profiles the operation of what has been referred to variously as 'private' or 'parallel' degree students in public universities. This is important for purposes of drawing comparative conclusions as to the degree to which public and private universities are responding to issues of equity and knowledge production. As noted in the case of private universities, the operations of privatising public universities are guided by the mission of the new programmes. This mission may sometimes complement and at others contradict the overall missions under which public universities were established in Kenya. The embedded public social responsibility of the universities has already been discussed in the introduction to this study. The initial missions of public universities emphasised the role of the universities in work force development and the creation of a socially equitable society. The new mission on the other hand emphasises the success of the universities in generating their own operating revenues through business-like practices in academia. In a sense, therefore we have a situation of two universities existing in one institution.

The first entails the remaining rudiments of a public university system. These are limited to students who are on partial or full government sponsorship. The number of students is limited to 10,000 every year selected from the best qualifying students from high schools. The students are centrally selected by the Joint Admissions Board, a committee of all public university vice-chancellors, and shared among all public universities proportionally. These are the students that are referred to as the 'module one' or 'regular' students. The other group consists of those students who are in the 'parallel' programme. Students in these programmes range from those pursuing certificate to postgraduate courses. Each university admits its own students and the criteria for admission vary from one university to another. Admission to academic programmes also varies across universities and criteria differ from those used to admit regular students into the same programmes. The admission of regular students is normally based on specific academic credits from high school. This bracket is considerably widened for the 'parallel' students in favour of ability to pay. In as much as the two categories of students are admitted based on different academic criteria and subjected to different institutional academic requirements, they constitute two different university models. The first model could be referred to as the 'public' university, while the second is the 'enterprise' or 'business' university.

The profile of modes of study in the 'parallel' programmes is broad and varies from one university to the other. Within one university, different groups of students may be pursuing the same programme. There are programmes where students are taught in the evenings and over weekends. The University of Nairobi, given its location within the capital city, is a popular destination for these groups of students. These students work and can only get time off in the evenings after work and at weekends. The university also admits full-time students who are integrated with the regular students. All these fee-paying students are admitted and coordinated under UNES, the corporate face of the university. The coordination of academic programmes and student evaluation for the 'parallel' students has also moved from the traditional academic departments to the corporate entity.

Kenyatta University, largely a teacher education institution, has a majority of the 'parallel' students during the holidays when schools close and teachers find time. The university integrates a few of the 'parallel' full-time students with regular students. However, it has recently bought a separate campus for the future development and growth of the parallel programmes. The university also has an institute of open learning for distance education programmes. In a different version, Kenyatta University of Agriculture and Technology accredits other diploma level institutions spread across the country to offer its programmes. This arrangement compensates for the lack of physical facilities at the institution to concentrate all the students. Egerton, Moi, and Maseno universities that are located in relatively rural parts of the country have bought buildings in nearby urban centres to attract the same cadre of students. All these arrangements influence the access of different groups of students to the institutions. The arrangements also alter the working environment of the faculty in terms of striking a balance between teaching and research. Two facts related to this came out during the study. One, the number of 'parallel' students in some universities such as Nairobi and Kenyatta was slightly more than the 'regular' ones. Two, in some professional programmes such as law, teaching and commerce, working student numbers were higher than those who were entering straight from high school.

Lastly, the distribution of revenues and profits accruing from the private programmes reflected certain contradictions. Privatising public universities was aimed at generating revenue to meet shortfalls from the government. The revenues were supposed to be used to improve the quality of university facilities and the general learning environment. Furthermore, lecturers could make extra money and compensate for the low salaries that they were paid. The thinking was that this would keep lecturers in the institutions and stem the brain drain, as they would be more available to their students. This has not entirely happened.

An analysis of the distribution of the revenues generated showed that utilisation was skewed away from core academic activities. For example at the University of Nairobi, ten percent of the revenue is budgeted for capital development projects, eight percent for teaching materials, three percent for office and teaching equipment, three percent for the purchase of journals and one percent for research grants. But forty-one percent is spent on salaries for service providers while UNES takes seven percent as a management fee. A substantial proportion of the revenues are evidently spent on staff welfare. This might be wise if their welfare was directly related to the business of the university. This is not the case. All the public universities in Kenya have a large proportion of their employees as support staff, even while some teaching departments do without enough lecturers. Given their large numbers, the non-teaching staff consume most of the revenue generated as emoluments, thus considerably reducing the amount going to lecturers and teaching facilities.

At Kenyatta University, five percent of the revenue is voted for research and the rest distributed unevenly based on the pressing issues at hand. Like Nairobi though, a large percentage goes to subsidise workers' emoluments. Because of this, the university has refused to enter into negotiation with the lecturers' union on the specific modalities of distributing income earned from the 'parallel' programmes. This has caused sporadic conflict between the union and the university administration that has occasionally led to the closure of the university. Generally, all the public universities are riddled with accusations of mismanagement and the pilfering of funds generated from the privatised programmes and students. Rather than being avenues to salvage the quality of the institutions, the programmes have opened a new front of conflict between university workers and management. These conflicts may continue to derail the objective of the programmes and the mission of the universities.

Conclusion

The evolution of private higher education and the privatisation of universities was a response to two developments. First was the increasing demand for higher education in the face of the financial inability of the government to expand admissions and subsidise students in public universities. This was a key impetus for the growth of private universities. Second was the desire by the management of public universities to stall the collapse of the institutions and reverse the decline in the quality of their programmes. By generating their own revenues and gaining financial autonomy from the government, the institutions could expand their facilities, increase access and improve remuneration of academic staff to stem the brain drain. The overall result would be institutions that responded well to their role as significant social institutions by striking a balance between expanding access and transmitting knowledge to students through teaching and to society through basic research. Privatising public university programmes was meant to achieve this objective. The discussion on the impact of privatisation and private higher education in this study was based on the perspective of these objectives.

The profiles of the four private universities that were included in the study bring out four issues that have implications for access and equity. First, the four universities are the oldest private institutions in the country. They command about 90 percent of student enrolment in private universities, apart from those in the private programmes of public universities. This critical factor influenced their selection for the study. Second, all these universities are foreign in origin, Daystar from USA, through Zimbabwe, CUEA, from Rome, through the Catholic Bishops of the East African region, USIU, from the US, and UEAB also from the US through the Adventist missions of the Middle East. Actually, all the private universities in Kenya are foreign owned except two. These are Kiriri Women's University of Science and Technology, and Kabarak University. Third, except for USIU, the other institutions covered by the study emphasise that they require observance of their religious beliefs as a condition for admission. This means the universities target a certain clientele based on religious affiliation in addition to the possession of academic qualifications. The religious orientation of the institutions could limit accessibility to students who do not realign themselves with the institutions' religious beliefs. The private universities also admit students from the East African region and the international market. This could limit the extent to which the institutions can design policies to address access and equity objectives in Kenya's higher education system. An even important point that directly relates to the discussion in the next section is the distinction between the for-profit and the not-for-profit private universities. Our research shows that the not-for profit status is limited to the registration legalities, and not to their actual operations. Institutions registered ostensibly as 'not-for-profit' in Kenya charge fees in the same range as the for-profit ones. The not-for-profit institutions also benefit from a financially endowed network of sponsors and the religiously faithful. Given this fact, one would expect the not-for-profit institutions not to engage in market like behaviour in the design and delivery of their programmes. One would also expect the institutions to widen the net in their admissions to include a substantial proportion of qualifying students who are excluded from university education based on inability to pay or other physical circumstances. These issues are raised in the following section of the study.

The private programmes of the public universities have been designed to generate money. The institutions are supposed to use the money generated to enhance the social responsibility of the institutions. Broadening access to students from all social groups who qualify for admission to university becomes a critical issue for the public universities. Admitting students on the ability to pay tends to exclude poor students who may be better qualified than those who can afford the fees. While lesser qualified fee-paying students might be considered acceptable in the purely private universities, their entry into public universities raises some interesting questions. The point has also been made that since Kenya does not have many university institutions, the few that exist have to combine their teaching and knowledge creation responsibilities. This will require a balance between the business-like and the social function of the universities on the one hand and the teaching and research function on the other. In the next section, the dynamics of access to the private universities and to the private programmes of public universities in Kenya are considered. The discussion is designed to highlight issues related to equity.

3

Dynamics of Access and Equity in Kenya's Private Universities and Programmes

Introduction: Conceptualising access and equity

Equity in education is often perceived solely in terms of the number of students gaining access to formal institutions of learning, and more so in terms of the enrolment rate at the first grade of the cycles of primary, secondary and tertiary education. However, this narrow conceptualisation tends to blur pertinent issues that hamper equity in the provision of educational opportunities. The principle that each citizen regardless of economic resources or personal traits deserves and has a right to equal treatment in a social system underlies the demand and support for social equity (Shafritz & Russell 2000). Within a human rights perspective, equity in education must encompass not only the concern for access, but also for participation (staying), performance (achievement of knowledge, skills and attitudes) as well as completion and transition to various benchmarks that determine the future of learners in the world of work as well as in social and personal development.

Because of the diverse ways in which the concept of 'equity' can be presented, misconceptions tend to emerge such that the idea of equity is tangled up with the broader concept of equality, creating confusion about which of the two concepts entails the other. In the context of this study, 'equity' is perceived as stemming from the sense of fairness and justice in the distribution of resources through a process that ensures that the rights of the majority and those of the minority are addressed accordingly and given 'equal' importance in enhancing the quality of human life. In this case, 'being fair and just' refers not so much to the issue of how the majority of the people attain or are accorded their rights, but rather to the conscious and deliberate attention to the extent to which the minority are also accorded, and enabled to pursue their rights as 'equal' human beings. Thus, equity becomes a temporary measure in ensuring that human beings benefit from state resources in a reasonable and relatively inclusive and sensitive manner.

At least two factors seem to explain why equity is an issue, not only in education but also in other sectors of social development. Firstly, observation reveals that conflicts and disputes in society emanate largely from socioeconomic inequality. The struggle over resources often forms the root of many conflicts and hostilities between and within nations. Secondly, there is a strong link between socioeconomic dominance on the one hand and political domination on the other. Thus, as wealthy nations dominate the poorer nations, within nations the wealthy citizens trample on the rights of the poor people, denying them the means for survival through the unfair distribution of the available resources. This macro practice is widely replicated within smaller social units such as family, where the family member who owns and controls the resources tends to also control its access and benefits, thus lording it over the dependants and determining their position and status in life. More often than not, gender relations have tended to determine the form and structure of dominance within the family, with the men according themselves the dominant role and relegating the women to subordinate positions. This gender arrangement has serious implications for women's access to national resources, including education, which is a key to other development gains.

In modern society, the overriding assumption is that some or all of inequality is wrong. Consequently, this assumption raises the fundamental question: What are the appropriate measures of redress in the face of inequality that result in social inequities? Should the concern for equity prevail over all other values in society or are there other important, if not overriding, social goals above equity values?

In addressing the above questions, it is important to underscore the fact that inequality, as a source of many forms of inequities, means that some individuals are favoured or privileged over others. Also important is the fact that systems that support social inequalities tend to justify their position by appealing to principles of entitlement and merit based upon equality of competition for opportunities. They argue that rewards should be linked to virtue, talent or contribution to society. This argument, typically founded on the liberal democratic traditions, though important and defensible as it appears, raises pertinent questions of morality. For example, if virtues, talent and contribution to society are all that count, is it right to ignore the process and social privileges upon which such talent, virtue and ability are developed and from which other less privileged persons may have been unfairly excluded? Is it not the case that the principle of merit, entitlement and privilege based on ideological positions appears invalid in the face of the empirical evidence? (See Denzin 1998: 139).

While in theory, treating people unequally may seem to be a bad thing (immoral), in addressing practical human concerns, the same treatment may have a different appeal that might even challenge us to consider whether all inequalities are morally wrong. Observations reveal the existence of perceived functional usefulness in some forms of inequalities that might be inevitable, if not morally imperative. Such inequalities are worth highlighting if they guide the process of justice or encourage the production of talent, which otherwise would be difficult to tap. In extreme cases, the defence of inequality borders on helping rid society of those who are naturally weak, lazy or unenterprising and thus supporting a world of 'survival of the fittest'.

Clearly, equity is a contested and often untidy concept whose essence lies, not in an event of distributing resources equitably, but also in the process of ensuring that all human beings will have an equal chance to enjoy the resources available. This renders the concern for justice and fair play a moral imperative in any meaningful debate on equity. Further, while equity is a difficult concept when confined to inequality within groups, it becomes even more problematic in respect of inequality between groups, thus problematising the concept by making it prone to a double standard of application. For instance, discrimination and inequality between groups is often far more objectionable than inequality within them. Notably, inequalities occasioned by racially motivated tendencies or practices such as apartheid tend to persistently provoke national and international condemnation, even from countries characterised by conspicuous and serious internal inequalities based on ethnic animosity or even gender discrimination. By contrast, inequality among individuals is often perceived to be 'natural'. Hence the form of inequality predominantly assumed natural is the one related to gender. Thus, women's social and cultural position is perceived to be socially necessary and rationalised as being closely associated with women's roles of rearing and caring.

In addition, other incidental features are conjured up and manifested in the domestication of the feminine which is then juxtaposed with the supposedly superior and 'free' masculine role that is considered to be in the interests of society, stable family life, proper childcare and, ultimately, of women themselves as dependants of men. This trend in social relations has resulted in the marginalisation of women, not just in their families but also in the wider society in terms of the distribution of, and access to, social benefits relative to men. This unequal distribution of resources translates into inequalities that manifest themselves in the relatively fewer numbers of women in positions of privilege, power, authority, control of resources and decision-making in the private domestic arena and the family as well as the public sphere of the labour market. However, it is important to remember that achieving gender equality is not just a question of balancing the numbers. It implies the provision of proper opportunities for learning and for benefiting from equitable treatment within the school, family and community as well as the same opportunities in terms of access to employment, wages earning and political participation.

Policy approaches to address equity issues in education are underpinned by particular contexts and traditions. In higher education, the manner in which institutional missions are articulated forms part of these contexts. A higher education system that gravitates towards the broadening of access and striking a balance between the interests of clients and broader social responsibility will articulate a liberal learning equity policy. In a context of market choice however, equity is likely to be narrowly conceived, exclusively in terms of the interests of individual clients. Miriam Henry (2001: 29-35) has conceptualised equity within this continuum. At the level of liberal individualism, there is a focus on ensuring that individuals have equal opportunities to access education. This approach aims at changing the social fortunes of individuals through education, not the culture that breeds their continued disadvantage. In the middle are social democratic policies that focus on the unequal distribution of social and economic benefits. Since these disadvantages are perpetuated through the educational system, equity policies aim to give more resources to disadvantaged groups as compensatory strategies. At the other extreme, market individualism policies that conceptualise equity within the requirements of a market-driven economy add to the negative impact that the culture of education and schools has on women. The emphasis here is not on social redistribution but on competition and individual entitlements. This approach does not take into account long-standing social and economic disadvantage.

This study focuses on both individual liberalism and market individualism as they influence access to private higher education in Kenya. The conceptualisation of the study is that amalgamating the two approaches can enhance the capacity of relevant organs to address equity concerns in Kenya's higher education system. An approach based on broadening access should be accompanied by a recognition of the cultural and economic disadvantages that are barriers to access and performance in education. A focus on socioeconomic differences should match a similar focus on the differences between social groups manifested in categories such as gender.

This conceptualisation ties in with the context of the evolution of private higher education in Kenya. It also takes into account the overall place of higher education in Kenya's development strategy. As has been argued elsewhere in this study, the impetus to the growth of private higher education in Kenya was the need to meet increasing demand. Students qualified to be admitted to university in Kenya come from all social groups, but the majority do not fall into the 'market choice' category, given the high levels of poverty in the country. The majority of the legally registered not-for-profit or demand-absorbing private universities therefore have to design policies of taking in students from all social groups. This is not an absurd expectation given that the institutions are self-financing and rely on student fees. With their religious orientation and their legal status, they have a moral imperative to address the socially excluded and price their courses with this consideration in mind. As noted in Section Two of this study, some of these universities benefit from a rich network of endowments and donations. The expectation therefore is that they should not fix their fees at such a level as to exclude a majority of the students and focus on small elite who are able to pay. However, more importantly, equity considerations require that a diversity of students forms the yardstick of even those institutions structured on market choice operations. The instructional process and the diversity of students should equally be the focus in the institutions as part of the practices to promote equity. This is because broadening of access and relaxed entry criteria mean that some students admitted to the institutions come from a background of low academic achievement and need more resources to compensate for their earlier disadvantages. In any case, the private universities that focus on market choice should strengthen their quality assurance processes as no market prospers with poorly developed skills.

The foregoing discussion shows the connection that there is between equity and quality. Providing access to individuals, groups and regions that would not have had access to higher education is one way of equalising opportunity. But expanding access should not translate into the provision of low quality education .This is important to note, as doubts are often cast on the quality of programmes in private higher education institutions, especially in Kenya. Perceptions that a private university offers cheap, market-driven, low capitalised courses contribute to this image. As Reehana (undated) notes, quality and access may be directly related in the sense that poor quality may be part of the explanation for why individuals fail to take up opportunities, or the reason why they fail to complete education programmes.

The subsequent parts of this section discuss the operations of private universities and private degree programmes concerning equity. The indicators used to analyse this include access and admission requirements. Specifically, access from marginal groups to the institutions is analysed. The groups are female students, students from poor or marginal regions of the country, the disabled, and students who require a second chance access.

Access and admission requirements

Access is the first critical factor in assessing how given institutions promote equity. In line with Article 26: 1 of the Universal Declaration of Human Rights, the principles of merit, capacity, efforts, perseverance and devotion demonstrated by those seeking entry should determine admission to higher education institutions (UNESCO 1998). A commitment to this notion of access requires that higher education institutions put in place mechanisms that facilitate the entry of the highest number of those who qualify, irrespective of gender, language, religion, economic and other socio-cultural considerations.

In this study, the key question was to establish whether private universities and programmes implement policies to expand access and give an equal chance to all qualifying students. Further, the study explores any implicit institutional regulations or requirements that may exclude some students. An analysis of the mission statements and the academic requirements for students to obtain admission to the private universities enables one to draw conclusions regarding this issue. Table 3.0 summarises the basic criteria for access to the four private universities.

The information summarised in Table 3.0 reveals three basic factors that to a degree influence access to the four private universities. The first is their mission statements that show the philosophies that underlie their academic programmes. Three universities, CUEA, UEAB, and Daystar, place some premium on the training of Christian men and women. There was no indication during fieldwork of any implicit limitation on non-Christian students from gaining access to the institutions. However, interviews with some students revealed that some were not at ease with the rigid Christian ethos that ordered the academic life and programmes of the institutions. Students interested in pursuing secular academic programmes would therefore be constrained in applying due to certain implicit religious expectations. In this regard, students and the public rated USIU favourably due to the secular nature of its programmes and operations.

Table 3.0: Access and admission requirements at four private universities in Kenya

Institution	Mission statement	Academic requirements	Catchment area
CUEA	Promote excellence in scientific research and service to enhance human and Christian living	C+ grade in secondary education and equivalent	National, regional and international
Daystar University	Equip Christian men and women to serve in supportive and leadership positions in various sectors in Africa	C+ grade at secondary education and equivalent	All African countries
UEAB	The provision and advancement of a holistic Christian quality education for the youth to equip them with the skills for service to God and mankind	C+ at secondary level and appropriate contribution	National and international
USIU	Build a humanistic approach through an education that will enable a person to meet the needs of the community through the acquisition of positive attitudes towards life	C+ grade at secondary level and equivalent	National and international

In terms of academic requirements, the four institutions have adopted uniform scholastic criteria, as standardised by the CHE. Indeed an overall grade of C+ at secondary certificate level is the minimum that a student requires to qualify for admission either to a public or to a private university in Kenya. Individual institutions enforce other requirements, but these only determine the academic programmes for which a student may registers, and do not limit gaining access to university. For example, USIU, in addition to the minimum aggregate grade for admission, uses the Maths and English scores as additional criteria for admission. The rationale for this policy is that since the majority of students are from different schools in Kenya that have different standards of instruction, their preparation for university education is far from uniform, K.C.S.E. results notwithstanding. Hence, all undergraduate students admitted to USIU are required to take placement exams in Maths and English. Again, USIU in this respect takes into consideration the prior academic disadvantage of students and provides extra resources to improve their performance.

In terms of the catchment area, all the private universities have taken a regional and international orientation, admitting students from outside Kenya. The charters for the institutions do not give guidance on the number of students they can admit from outside the country. This may raise issues concerning the commitment of the institutions to their demand-absorbing role, and the interests of the country in which they are located. A situation where they may decide, for whatever reason, to accept more of their students who are non-Kenyan has not been foreseen by the regulatory authorities. This is a positive development given the internationalisation of higher education and the need to expose students to a diversity of cultures. However, the positive aspect of this should be analysed against two related contexts:

(i) The growing number of Kenyans who do not have access to higher education, and for whom private higher education offered locally should make provision;
(ii) The fact that by opening admission to regional and international students when the demand in Kenya is not satisfied may mean the exclusion of qualified Kenyan students. This is because where tuition fees are charged at market unit costs, regional and international students from stable socioeconomic backgrounds might have an advantage over Kenyan students.

Lastly, all the universities peg admission to payment of fees. Failure to raise the initial registration fees means that one forfeits one's place. At the UEAB and USIU, late payment of any fees attracts interest charges. The daily interest charge at USIU is 1.5 percent of the average daily balance of the student's account. All the private universities also levy other charges that push the cost of academic programmes higher than the official tuition fees. For example, while USIU officially charges an annual fee of Ksh 137,924 (US$ 2,682), other charges include a host of items such as boarding and meals, medical, transport, laboratory and computer application and graduation fees, which amount to Ksh 192,220 (US$ 2,563). This sum is more than the annual tuition fee. At CUEA, the annual tuition fee quoted is Ksh 138,240 (US$ 1,843), while the other charges average Ksh 12,270 (US$ 1,637). Daystar with official tuition fees of Ksh 164,000 (US$ 2,187), levies other charges that total Ksh 110,800 (US$ 1,477), Ksh 87,000 (US$ 1,160) of which is a mandatory payment. Again, these fees fluctuate depending on a student's field of specialisation. Students in science-based courses pay slightly more than indicated here. These comparisons demonstrate two points. Students could only afford the cumulative fees charged by the private institutions if they either are from wealthy backgrounds or enjoy sponsorship. This has continued to maintain private universities as elite institutions catering for the interests of those able to meet the fees. Two, contrary to their 'not-for-profit' legal status, the predominant faith-based institutions charge fees as high as the for-profit institutions. The comparison with fees charged by USIU a secular for-profit institution, and the other religious institutions, is telling in this respect. The missions of the private universities that stress either religious background and ability to pay do not encompass an agenda of opening up the institutions to students from marginal groups who qualify for university but are constrained by financial ability. Indeed none of the universities has an explicit policy regarding equity, including gender – something that the private universities have indicated their desire to excel in addressing.

These observations are critical in drawing conclusions on how the development of private higher education in Kenya has significantly expanded access and addressed equity. One way to address this issue is to look at the proportion of students admitted to private universities from the absolute number of students who qualify for admission to universities annually. The second level is to analyse the demographic profiles of students admitted to private universities to establish if and how they cater for students from marginal groups.

The rate of expansion in the private universities has been rather slow. Even if they were to retain their elite status, there are many more qualifying students with the ability to pay who are not finding placement in the private universities of their choice and at a time that they want to register. This is happening even as the demand for university places keeps increasing each year. The growth in student enrolment in the private universities has not been dramatic in this respect, save for the period before the introduction of private programmes in public universities. For example, the five accredited universities (the four covered in this study, plus Scott Theological College), enrolled 5,210 students in the 1996–1997 academic year (see Table 2.0). This number increased to 7,143 students in the 2000–2001 academic year, 7,639 in 2002–2003, 8,021 in 2003–2004 and 8,342 in 2004–2005. In absolute terms, these figures represented an increase of 6.49 percent, 4.76 percent and 3.8 percent in the respective academic years. Perhaps a more accurate picture can emerge from the comparison of the total number of students who qualify for university admissions.

In the year 2003, 207,730 candidates sat the Kenya Certificate of Secondary Education. About 50,000 of these candidates qualified for admission to university. The public universities admitted only 10,000 qualifiers only – 20 percent of the total eligible. Private universities admitted only 3,000 – six percent (JAB Statistics 2004). Indeed, while the total number of students enrolled in public universities averaged 55,200 in the 2004–2005 academic year, those in private universities combined averaged 10,000 in the same period (*East African Standard*, 8 April 2004). By 2005, public universities enrolled 81,491 public students, while the 17 private universities admitted 10,050 students (JAB Statistics). Overall, the figures of those admitted represent only 0.3 percent of the total population. There continues therefore to be a large unmet market for higher education in Kenya that the institutions are not meeting. This shows that private universities, despite the positive approval that society has accorded them, have not matched these expectations at a rate of expansion to meet growing demand. This has tended to limit access of eligible students, thus undermining equity considerations.

Even if one were to accept the market logic and agree that the private universities can only admit students with the capacity to pay, one cannot understand why the pace of expansion has been too slow to address this group of students. The private universities covered by this study indicated that they receive more applications from qualified students than they could admit. Consequently, each of the institution has a number of students on the waiting list for admission. There is also no explicit policy in the institution to admit qualified Kenyans first, although in any one admission Kenyans outnumber the total number of foreign students accepted. At USIU, only 66 percent, 80 percent, 76 percent, 77 percent and 83 percent of total applicants were admitted in the years 2000, 2001, 2002, 2003 and 2004 respectively (USIU, 'Data elements to support the capacity and preparatory review report', 2005). Within the same period, about ten percent of the students at the institution fell into the foreign enrolment category. Such a slow pace, although not stated in any official policy, may be a consequence of the market logic that dictates the operations of the institutions.

The total numbers of students enrolled in the private universities are thus not exclusively from Kenya. All the four private universities covered in this study attested to admitting students from the international market. As earlier noted, this causes concern as students from strong economies provide undue competition to Kenyan students when certain market principles, such as the ability to pay tuition fees, defines who gets admission first. This concern is justified given that the pressure to establish and regulate private universities stemmed from the growing demand from Kenyans for higher education.

The achievement of equity through broadening access to private universities in Kenya seems to be constrained by three factors. Significantly, the private institutions do not operate on any stated and broadly defined equity policies. Two the institutions have not expanded fast enough to match the demand for places. Consequently, many qualified applicants have to wait for some time to get admission, thereby replicating the problem at public universities, where students have to wait for a year or so before admission. The admission of international students, some from economically strong backgrounds, may be edging out Kenyan students, especially from economically disadvantaged groups.

The slow pace in the expansion of private higher education in Kenya thus poses some questions. The questions revolve around the hesitation of the sector to expand in the face of demand and the continuing focus on a small elite. Some of the elite students are foreigners. Some are Kenyans working for international corporations. In addition, others are Kenyans who have placed their hopes of a better education and job on these private universities. It is in this respect that, like the import substitution industries, some private universities are perfecting the internationalisation of higher education.

The private programmes in public universities admit students based on ability to pay and academic qualifications. Since the aim of the programmes is to generate income for the universities, there is no consideration of non-fee paying students. Most students in the programmes are either working people or those who are able to marshal individual and family resources to pay the tuition fees.

The socioeconomic background of students in private universities and programmes

The achievement of equity requires that institution put in place policies to facilitate access to higher education institutions for students who qualify, but cannot enrol due to socioeconomic circumstances. The literature on the growth of private higher education cites the diversity of students seeking admission, and the increasing diversity of economic skills required in the market as part of the driving forces for the growth of private university institutions. Hence, it is reasonable to expect that diversity in demand should be marched with diversity in supply. This is important, as diversity of students is a mark of the quality of institutions even within marketised higher education systems.

Institutions can promote diversity among students in several respects. One is through sourcing scholarships, grants, and bursaries for qualified students from poor backgrounds. Some institutions set aside a percentage of their revenue for this purpose. The second strategy is through institutions offering graduated tuition fees for some category of students. Faith-based institutions that have other sources of finance can take this step for students from poor socioeconomic backgrounds. This means a percentage of poor but qualified students are admitted and the institutions either waive or subsidise shortfalls in their tuition fees, in the spirit of corporate social responsibility. Thirdly, institutions can have work-study schemes that target students from poor families. This possibility should entail a systematic profiling of students from high school to ensure that such schemes benefit deserving students only. In doing so, private universities would be perceived not only to be working on market principles, but also to be striving towards the achievement of social equity.

In Kenya, good quality secondary education and access to competitive faculties in higher education are influenced by the differential socioeconomic endowments that characterise the different regions of the country. Rich regions have managed to develop high quality education facilities and the cultural capital that determines quality. The primary and secondary schools in these regions produce students with high grades that ensure them access to the best-subsidised university education. To have a grasp of how inclusive or exclusive access to higher education is requires an understanding of how these dynamics of access actually work. Kenya also has a well-developed private primary education sector. Every year private primary schools eclipse public ones in examination performance. Of course, children of the poor cannot afford the expensive but high quality education offered in these private schools. Consequently, children from rich families who go to private schools end up taking places in the best public national and provincial secondary schools. This system has, over time, made access to the professional faculties in public universities a preserve of a group of students from rich families. The emergence of a private higher education sector that offers a narrowly conceived curriculum and pegs admission on ability to pay can only make a bad situation worse.

Public universities now operate two systems. There is the public one where students admitted are those that qualify through higher marks from high school. Tuition fees for these students are heavily subsidised by the government. The second system embraces the fee-paying students. Given the dynamics of secondary school selection, the majority of students who end up at the public universities under public subsidies are those from rich backgrounds who went to good public secondary schools via private primary schools. Private universities also target this group of students whose families have the capacity to meet tuition expenses. This means that a majority of qualifying students who do not have immediate alternatives are from modest economic backgrounds. They include students from Kenya's arid regions with a low economic potential and consequently a situation of educational underdevelopment. According to statistics from JAB, which regulates student admission to public universities, this trend still prevails. Table 3.1 summarises information related to the admission to public universities of students from different socioeconomic clusters in Kenya. The information shows the small number of students from the weaker socioeconomic regions of the country who are admitted to public universities.

Table 3.1: Public university admissions from disadvantaged (ASAL) regions as a percentage of the national intake

Years		No. Registered for KCSE	No. Eligible for admission (C+)	No. Selected
1998	Disadvantaged regions	10,036	1,479	370
		169,357	30,243	8,150
	National percentage	5.3%		4.0%
2000	Disadvantaged regions	9,597	1,796	449
		178,608	40,491	11,147
	National percentage	5.3%	4.4%	4.0%
2002	Disadvantaged regions	11,298	1,974	437
		198,076	42,720	10,923
	National percentage	5.7%	4.6%	4.0%

Source: Report of the JAB sub-committee on review of admission criteria, May 2005

From Table 3.1, it is evident that students from economically disadvantaged regions have a lower chance of gaining admission to university. The number of districts (regions) in Kenya classified as ASAL due to their low economic potential and geographical location constitutes over one third of the total. This situation therefore affects a significant proportion of Kenya's population. The ASAL regions not only register an insignificant number of students for the Form Four university entrance examination (an average of five percent), but also only provide an average of four percent of those students actually obtaining admission to university.

An analysis of responses from student questionnaires and records shows that private universities and programmes have accentuated the above trend. Strikingly, none of the private universities kept an up-to-date education management system profiling the socioeconomic and regional backgrounds of their students. The religious based private universities reflected this failure in their missions. Since they were religious institutions, profiling of students is discouraged on the grounds of avoiding putting artificial distinctions on human beings who are 'equal in God's eyes'. The institutions interpreted the practice positively as one aimed at promoting 'equality' among students. The universities put a higher premium on the ability of students to pay tuition fees over everything else. Though private universities have some tuition support programmes, they do not have a clear criterion to ensure that admission of students redressed the regional imbalances that have been a major source of regional human capital inequalities and social inequality in Kenya. The responses from CUEA summarised in Table 3.2 largely reflect the regional profiles of students in public and private universities in Kenya

Table 3.2: Regional representation of students at CUEA, 2003

Region	No.	%	% Within national population
North Eastern	0	0	0.3
Eastern	12	16.4	16
Central	14	19.2	13
Western	14	19.2	12
Coast	1	1.4	9
Rift Valley	12	16.4	7
Nyanza	13	17.8	15
Nairobi	7	9.6	25
Total	73	100	100

Source: compiled from field data.

Table 3.2 corroborates the information in Table 3.1 that most students in private universities come mainly from the better-off economic regions of the country. These same areas have traditionally benefited from the quality of educational provision. By extrapolation therefore, and since private universities insist on registration first before any financial assistance is arranged for needy students, most students who access private universities and programmes are from middle and high socioeconomic backgrounds. In addition, a sizeable proportion of students admitted to private universities and programmes are actually working and can raise their tuition fees from salaries. At USIU, the largest private university, about 30 percent of students were in part-time evening classes because they had to work during the day.

Most students enrolled in the private programmes of public universities are in formal employment. Many of these students attend their programmes in the evenings, over the weekends and during the holidays (for teachers). The private students raise fees from various sources. There are those who are sponsored by their employers. Others use personal savings and loans with their salaries as collateral. This means that the majority of the private working students afford the tuition fees charged by the universities with ease. For example, at the University of Nairobi, a record 244 students graduated with an MBA degree in 2003. Out of this, only 50 were regular students, whereas the rest were privately sponsored (University of Nairobi, Graduation Booklet, 2003). At the University's Parklands Law Campus, only 600 students were registered as regular against 1,400 privately sponsored students in 2004. This illustrates a trend where public universities are limiting the number of regular students to professional courses to create more space for those with the ability to pay.

At Kenyatta University, the second largest public university, and the largest teacher training institution in the region, the trend is the same. Most of the courses are tailor-made for serving teachers, and possession of a professional certificate is a requirement for admission. These admission policies are more suited to students who are working and therefore constitute a middle and high SES class. The working students also take more places in the professional courses. Whereas public universities have reduced the number of students admitted to regular programmes, citing resources and space as constraints, they admit double the number of private students to the same programmes, without citing any constraining factors as long as the students pay.

The increasing privatisation of programmes in public universities is good for the financial stability of the institution. However, the developments are not tenable from an equity perspective. A majority of the students now being admitted under the private category did not in the first place qualify to enter university competitively. However, with privatisation, they can be admitted not only to public universities but also to competitive professional faculties like medicine, law and engineering whose tuition fees are much higher. This disadvantages students from poor backgrounds who cannot be admitted to such professional courses even with better grades. Students from rich backgrounds, who score say a grade B- from high school and cannot be admitted to professional courses under the regular category, eventually enrol in the same courses through the private programmes.

Another contradiction exists. Students who join private programmes in public universities do not access loans from the Higher Education Loans Board (HELB). However, those in purely private universities are allowed to access these loans. HELB is a public body capitalised through public funds. To allow one section of private students to access such funds while locking out others is a clear manifestation of inequity. The assumption here is that since private programmes in public universities were started to generate money, students who apply for them are well-to-do. The same argument could be used for those in purely private universities. This reasoning is however ignored. Economically disadvantaged students who enrol in the private programmes of public universities are in this case excluded from accessing tuition loans while their counterparts in the private universities from rich backgrounds get consideration. Such admission procedures contribute to widening social inequalities in the broader social context.

Equity objectives can be undermined by the amount of tuition and other fees that institutions charge. Some of these charges have been discussed above. The slow growth of student numbers in private universities may be a pointer to the fact that the amount of tuition fees charged can be afforded only by a few of the elite.

Data on students who had dropped out due to non-payment of fees were not available at any of the universities. Private universities insisted on fee payment well in advance of commencement of studies. The profile of students in private universities as a small elite from economically advantaged backgrounds, some working in international organisations, implies a clientele with not only the capacity but also the culture of paying upfront for services. The clientele is absolved by circumstances, from the working class mentality of protracted negotiations and delayed payments. This does not however mean that private universities do not have financially deserving students. But they would constitute the minority and their level of need might be minimal.

At the public universities, it was difficult to confirm which students had dropped out due to lack of finances and which had taken time off due to reasons unrelated to finance. The picture created was that private universities and programmes in public universities were going on well. Students were being admitted based on their ability to pay and more were willing. The limitation was the capacity of the institutions that was not expanding. This however could be misleading.

As already, indicated public universities admit about 20 percent of qualified students annually. Another 15–20 percent would be entering through the private programmes. With an annual growth in student intakes averaging four percent, the private universities combined admit 15 percent straight from high school and five percent as continuing education students. The overall picture formed by this study is that 60 percent of the students who qualify to enter universities straight from high school in Kenya are not placed. This is the number that explains the different facets of inequity in higher education in Kenya. Table 3.3 is a comparative summary of the average annual tuition fees paid in private universities and private programmes in public universities at the time of the study. The Table serves to illustrate further that despite their different registration statuses all private universities and programmes in public universities shared in the commercial motive in their academic offerings.

Table 3.3: Average annual undergraduate tuition fees in private universities and programmes in Kenya

Institution	Average Annual Fees					
	Arts-based courses		Science-based courses		Competitive professional courses, e.g. medicine	
	Ksh	US$	Ksh	US$	Ksh	US$
USIU	189,936	2,532.48	200,636	2,675	-	
CUEA	138,240	1,843.2	162,000	2,160	-	
UEAB	217,000	2,893	217,000	2,893	-	
Daystar	164,000	2,187	184,000	2,453	-	
Kenyatta	100,000	1,333	120,000	1,600		
Nairobi	80,000	1,066	320,000	4,266	500,000	6,666

Source: compiled from field data. The Table is a summary of average tuition fees. Other charges such as meals, accommodation and transport have not been included. The professional courses such as medicine, actuarial sciences, engineering and computer technology are offered at the universities of Nairobi, Moi, and Jomo Kenyatta University of Agriculture and Technology. One US Dollar = 75 Kenyan shillings.

It is evident from the table that average annual tuition fees in private universities and programmes in public universities range from US$ 2,000 to US$ 2,500 per student. Tuition fees for professional courses in public universities begin at around US$ 6,000. According to the Government of Kenya Economic Statistics (2003), about 60 percent of Kenyans live in poverty, 49 percent of whom are in the rural areas. Given these poverty levels among most of the population, the range of fees charged by private higher education institutions would be too high for most qualified Kenyans. The annual income even for the majority of salaried Kenyans does not exceed US$ 2,400. Since charges in the Table have not taken into account other expenses, it is practically impossible for most families, even from the average working class, to access private higher education. This partly explains the continuing low intake of students to private universities that has averaged six percent of the total qualifiers over the years. The general picture here is that the access of new regular students to private higher education institutions and programmes that have been marketised is severely limited. The use of ability to pay as a key admission requirement to private higher education has both quality and equity implications. Students from rich backgrounds are using money to buy university education they do not deserve or need in the first place at the expense of those from poor backgrounds to whom education is the only available avenue for social mobility.

Private universities operate work-study and other student financial aid schemes. For example at Daystar University, students could work on campus for ten hours a week and earn up to Ksh 60,000 (US$ 800) a semester as tuition fees. At UEAB, a student could earn up to Ksh 2,500 (US$ 33) per month, which is credited to the student's tuition account. At the USIU, the financial aid office organises students to get financial assistance for their academic or professional programmes. However, the operation of the work-study programmes and student financial aid schemes does not necessarily promote equity or target deserving students. Students who would be considered are those that have already joined the institutions. This means one has to raise the initial registration and maybe a semester's fees. Students from poor families may not have this option. In other words to obtain any mode of financial assistance in the private universities you have to offer some proof of financial ability, a contradiction in this respect. The religious leaning private universities add other considerations for students who wish to be considered for tuition support. The policy of the universities is that awards are made on the basis of academic achievement and financial need. Character and leadership references indicative of one's commitment to the university and active commitment to one's faith' are added crucial considerations.

Overall, the total numbers of students benefiting from financial aid schemes are few in all the universities and the amount of tuition support is graduated, depending on the perceived level of need. At UEAB, the study team was given a list of 120 students who were engaged in work-study programmes. The university does not have a policy of direct tuition support. At USIU, an average of ten percent of the undergraduate students enrolled receive some tuition support each academic year. Students in the private programmes of public universities are not entitled to any form of tuition support either from the institutions or from the government. Generally, the dynamics through which tuition support operate exclude qualified students from poor backgrounds. This significantly contributes to inequities throughout private higher education. Regardless of their self-financing and commercial leanings, private higher education institutions should plough some of the income they generate into the communities. Assisting qualified but poor students could perhaps be the best way for the institutions to integrate a public service component into their operations.

Gender equity in higher education: Focusing beyond the classroom

The fact that both social and private returns to investment in education are not equal but also slightly higher for girls than boys is generally accepted the world over. Returns to investment in women's education and health are significantly greater than for similar investment in men, largely because of the strong interaction of women's education, health and nutritional status, and fertility levels and their effect on the education, health and productivity of future generations. Research demonstrates that at a social level investing in the female human capital resource will generate important benefits for society in the form of lower child mortality, higher educational attainment, better nutrition, and slower population growth. In addition, evidence abounds that under-investment in women's education limits domestic productivity and hampers other social and developmental gains, including family health, political action and personal growth. Since the early 1990s, it has been established that education for women may yield the highest return of all investment available in developing countries, considering both private benefits and returns to other family members (World Bank 2004). Logically then, the perpetuation of gender inequalities can only increase inefficiencies that retard national growth, in terms both of human capital and of economic productivity.

Surprisingly, but nonetheless true, the total earnings of women amount, on average to 30 to 40 percent less than those of men (World Bank 2004). Hence, it is not surprising that fewer women than men participate in the labour force. A vicious circle ensues as households invest less in daughters than in sons in the belief that investment in girls yields fewer benefits. As a result, many women in Kenya do not get a useful education, and hence do not work outside the household as salaried workers because, evidently, they lack the relevant education, skills and experience that many of the men have.

Discrimination in households and in the labour market carries not only private costs for individuals and households but also social costs for society. This is despite the fact that the decision for women not to participate in the labour force does not necessarily reflect the woman's own choice, nor does it always correspond to the optimum use of household resources. Rather, it is a function of shortcomings in the attention given to the process of ensuring that women and men, in their differences and similarities, are enabled to acquire the education that they deserve.

Typically, most women have the responsibility for non-wage household work, such as childcare, food preparation, and, in low-income countries especially, subsistence farming and the collection of wood for fuel and water. The decision to allocate women's time to these activities has less to do with economics than with social conventions and norms. Even in the industrialised economies, where women's average levels of human capital are equal to, and sometimes higher than, those of men, women perform the bulk of household work. Whether this division of labour is appropriate is, essentially, for society to appraise and react to. Undoubtedly, education and employment for women, as a group, is often affected directly by the extensive amounts they devote to household maintenance and family care. Research reveals that most men do not allocate similar amounts of time to the home. Consequently, the inequalities of time allocation of the household division of labour constrain women's employment choices and often limit girls' benefits from schooling. Ultimately, the economy pays for this inequality through reduced labour productivity and diminished future national outputs.

The causes of the persistent inequalities between men and women are complex. Firstly, many governments do not seem to prioritise the causes of the status quo beyond mere rhetoric. Secondly, social institutions, particularly the family, school and community, tend to reinforce rather than deconstruct gender boundaries, thus helping to perpetuate the foundation of gender inequalities. Because of this, few societies in the world accord women the same opportunities as men. Often, the women work longer hours and are paid less, both in total and proportionately. In addition, their time, in both work and leisure, is much more constrained than for men. These disparities generate substantial gaps between how much women and men can contribute to society and, respectively, how much they share in accrued benefits. In most countries, a fundamental aspect of these disparities, which is both one of their causes and one of their continuing consequences, is inequality in access to and performance in education, right from primary schooling to higher learning. Of concern is the current tendency to emphasise equity of access for girls and boys at primary level as a quick fix for gender disparities in higher education while little is done to ensure that the majority of girls survive the lower levels of schooling. This serves to expose the lack of holistic approaches that would account for continuity and successful transition of both the girls and the boys to higher levels of learning. Because the ensuing educational inequalities are so deep-seated, surmounting them within the individual levels of education is bound to continue failing.

Essentially, the continuing prevalence of educational inequality, particularly at higher levels of learning, should serve as an important indicator of serious problems pertaining to gender issues at the lower levels of education. While countries of the world have pledged to eliminate gender disparities in primary and secondary education by 2005, this attainment remains a mirage for many of them. This situation tends to validate the doubts raised by UNESCO (2004) regarding the possibility of achieving equity in higher education in the near future.

The education sector, particularly in the developing countries, and more so in sub-Saharan Africa, is bogged down with serious problems ranging from declining enrolment rates at the different levels, reduced investments per learner, erosion of quality of education and low levels of student achievement. In all these problems, gender disparities are highly pronounced at the university level where only less than a third of all enrolled students are female. Although over the years this region has recorded rising trends of female as a percent of total enrolment, it is noteworthy that much of this progress has been apparent mainly at the primary level where government subsidies and support from the international donor community has done much to increase universal primary enrolment levels. However, these gains hardly translate into increases in university education for girls and women. Due to unfavourable circumstances as expounded in this study, the fate of most girls and women in higher education in sub-Saharan countries seems to have been sealed right from primary school and even from their homes and communities. Enrolment trends of around 45 percent at the primary level and only 40 percent at the secondary, are just but one confirmation of what is to be expected at university where men have dominated and continue to dominate and benefit from higher education (World Bank 1995). In this context then, it is fair to argue that attempts to enhance gender equity at university are bound to remain a theoretical luxury as long as gender equity issues are dislocated from the broader discourse of deconstructing the many sites of inequality, all of which interact with formal education at various levels.

Privatising higher education in Kenya: A slap in the face for gender equity

Firstly, it is worthwhile to ask whether private or public universities have remained a preserve for the development of male human capital. Secondly, the privatisation of higher education does not necessarily help improve gender equity but may rather help to enhance the existing socioeconomic gaps by enabling both the girls and boys from wealthy families to participate in the commercialised institutions of learning. Although statistics may indicate that private universities have a relatively better female-male ratio compared with public universities, the national ratio continues to underscore the fact that, as a group, women continue to be locked out of higher education. First, it should be pointed out that private universities and programmes in public universities do not operate with any explicit gender policy concerning their admission procedures. This is despite their operations in a national and international context that require affirmative responses to redress gender inequities in resource allocation.

In Kenya, women constitute over 50 percent of the population but 70 percent of those who live in poverty (Republic of Kenya 2004). According to this report, female enrolment averaged 49 percent, 48.2 percent, and 30.8 percent in public primary, secondary and tertiary levels respectively in 2004. The share of female students in private universities was 54.5 percent from an absolute enrolment of 8,021 students. Redressing this situation requires proactive policies that should guide institutions in their admission and conduct of academic programmes. In so doing, private higher education would be enhancing, not diminishing, its long-term commercial interests. Building a strong female social capital now in countries with higher female populations would widen the client base of higher education in the future. Public universities have adopted policies on affirmative actions in favour of increasing female education. Over the years, the policy has enabled female students to be admitted to the public universities at one point lower than their male colleagues. This policy however does not benefit students in the private programmes of public universities. The affirmative policy also does not influence the admission of female students to competitive professional faculties.

The private universities and programmes do not operate on any affirmative action policies – or gender policy for that matter. Private universities and programmes function on a commercial basis and have no formal mechanism to address the issue of gender in admissions. Private programmes in public universities also have this limitation. Hence, it would be incorrect to claim that the mission of private universities and programmes is to enhance gender equity because logic demonstrates that only rich families can afford to register their children at such institutions. It is also insincere for the private universities to claim that they are addressing the issue of gender inequities in higher education.

Table 3.4: Student enrolment by gender in public and private universities in Kenya, 1999–2000 to 2003–2004

Institution	1999–2000		2000–2001		2001–2002		2002–2003		2003–2004	
	M	F	M	F	M	F	M	F	M	F
Public universities										
Nairobi	8,419	3,523	10,532	4,302	15,426	9,270	16,200	9,486	16,991	9,720
Kenyatta	4,188	3,008	5,942	4,010	6,831	4,984	10,737	4,998	10,753	5,023
Moi	3,483	2,312	4,753	3,766	5,469	3,869	6,275	4,549	5,804	4,643
Egerton	7,131	2,842	6,629	2,356	6,816	2,284	6,975	2,387	6,908	2,444
Jomo Kenyatta	2,511	626	2,992	1,288	2,565	1,115	3,184	1,404	3,203	1,454
Maseno	2,338	1,385	2,596	1,538	2,531	1,518	3,505	2,130	3,429	2,178
Subtotal	28,070	13,696	33,444	17,260	39,637	23,040	4,6875	24,957	47,088	25,462
Private Universities										
Private accredited	3,186	3,816	3,093	4,050	3,122	4,089	3,476	4,163	3,650	4,371
Private not accredited	777	346	876	472	949	511	748	742	763	757
Subtotal	3,963	4,162	3,969	4,522	4,071	4,600	4,224	4,905	4,413	5,128
Total	32,003	17,858	37,412	21,782	43,708	27,640	51,099	29,862	51,501	30,590
Grand total	49,891		59,194		71,348		80,961		82,091	

Enrolment in public universities includes those in private degree programmes. All enrolments include students enrolled in non-degree programmes.
Source: Ministry of Education, Science and Technology.

The higher percentage of female students registered in the private universities and programmes however needs to be explained. First, more female students are shut out of public universities annually. This is due to a combination of factors that have been alluded to earlier. More female students are in provincial rural schools that do not have adequate resources and a small percentage of these students obtain places in public universities competitively. Clearly more of them would seek admission to private universities – that is, if they can afford to pay the exorbitant fees and not because of any affirmative action. The bottom line is that such girls are paying more to attain higher education. Indeed, one of the arguments put forward during the time of this study by private universities was that in a culture that marginalises women, the enrolment of female students was more than male students in most of their programmes. This is not however a consequence of any formal institutional policy or practice that encourages the enrolment of female students. Second, private universities offer most courses in the Arts and Humanities. These courses have not only been feminised but are cheaper. The high enrolment of female students in private universities can therefore be a source of perpetuating gender inequities given the curricula of the institutions that shepherd women into traditional feminine disciplines that attract lower remuneration in the job market.

It is evident from Table 3.4 that private universities enrol a higher number of female than male students, although in absolute terms there are more female students in public universities than there are in private universities. However, as already discussed, the institutions do not have any institutional policies to promote the higher enrolment of female students. Students just happen to enrol and more of them happen to be women. In this regard, it should be noted that public universities have tried to redress this situation through a series of affirmative action strategies. It should also be noted that analysis within individual public universities reveals a tendency where more women enrol in certain disciplines that have traditionally been considered 'soft' and amenable to the female gender. For example, Jomo Kenyatta University of Agriculture and Technology attracts few female students due to its purely practical science orientation in terms of courses offered.

Admission of students to the private programmes shows up another important development. At the University of Nairobi, the enrolment of female students in some of the private programmes is sometimes more, in others almost at par, with male students. For example, this study established that female students comprised 45 percent of the enrolments in the MBA programme in the 2003–2004 academic year. The ratio of female to male students in the faculty of medicine was 55:45 in the same period. An expanded vision of equity in terms of women accessing professional courses is therefore realised more through the private programmes of public universities. This is due to the diversity of their programmes. The higher enrolment of female students in private universities was also not unique to these institutions. It is happening in Kenya in institutions that tend to offer more of what are perceived to be 'traditionally female' academic disciplines. By popularising their programmes on a narrowly conceived gender equity perspective, private universities are in fact contributing to gender inequity in terms of human capital endowments. This they do by channelling women into academic and professional courses that do not give them an edge in the labour market (both in terms of the relative perception of value of knowledge and skills acquired, and wage structures).

While it might be assumed that women and men are free to enter higher education institutions and to pursue studies equally, empirical evidence of the actual practice disproves such an assumption. The history of the rise of universities embracing Greek, Roman and Islamic civilisation offers little evidence of women being accorded equal rights to education with men, let alone university education, private or public. Examples of struggles for gender equity in higher education are cited in studies dating way back to the rise of medieval universities and scholasticism, where graduate students and 'masters' were exclusively male (perhaps explaining the title 'master', which in the English language denotes maleness). Apparently women did not enjoy the privilege of attaining such high levels of education and even at lower levels, they could only learn under private tutors or nuns, thus denying them public education and competition in the institutions of higher learning. In medieval Europe, for example, the university started as a 'community' of scholars all men, with the authority to confer degrees. Despite the actual origins of these earliest universities being obscure, available records indicate that students who were sent to university at a much younger age than is now customary were only boys. The girls were kept out. As university education flourished during the Middle Ages, it was not generally encouraged for women. However, wealthy household were able to employ poor university students as tutors and on such occasions, girls were sometimes permitted to join the tutoring sessions of their brothers. Such historical scenarios provide a fair reflection of contemporary private universities, in which only girls from wealthy parents have equal privilege to higher education alongside boys and men from similar socioeconomic backgrounds.

Instructive examples derived from experience as recently as the beginning of the twentieth century in Europe (the major coloniser of the African continent) reveal just how difficult it was for women to acquire university education. In England, for instance, the women themselves pioneered their agenda to enter higher education amidst considerable resistance from the men. By the nineteenth century, a few women such as Emily Davies, Josephine Butler, Selina Billington Greig, and Eleanor Sidgewick agitated for university education for women and argued vehemently that without a university degree it was very difficult for women to enter the professions. After lengthy struggles that spanned the nineteenth and early twentieth century, the medical profession allowed women to become doctors. Even then, by 1900, there were only 200 women doctors in England and it was not until 1910 that women were allowed to become accountants and bankers. As a practical demonstration of commitment to female higher education, Emily Davies and Barbara Bodchon helped set up Girton University College for women in Cambridge in 1870 (Spartacus Educational 2001). A decade later in 1880, Eleanor Sidgewick set up Nenham College, yet another women's only college in Cambridge of which she became the principal. However, even with these bold strides by women educationalists, the university authorities treated the colleges with suspicion and even refused to recognise Girton College. In addition, as if to add insult to injury, the University of Cambridge did not accord degrees to women until the mid-twentieth century.

What these English women did was to try to locate women's roles within changing gender dynamics that required a balance between the private and public arenas where men and women interacted in social and economic development. They exposed as unfounded the fear that most men of their time (and many of today) tend to harbour against women entering higher education. These examples drawn from the history of women's university education in the land of the former colonisers of the African continent do not reveal any substantive differences from the experience of higher education for contemporary African women whose educational careers often collapse before they can set foot in a university. Since universities in sub-Saharan Africa derive their traditions from histories of colonisation that devalued education for women right from the early stages, it would be foolhardy to expect contemporary educational practices to deviate in any significant way.

Undoubtedly, African governments have taken long to acknowledge the enormity of educational injustices committed against women and the need to redress them decisively. The gains of this realisation that have been achieved through affirmative action are being eroded with similar zeal through the privatisation of higher education. Currently, many African governments have put in place policies of affirmative action as the humane way of righting past wrongs and thus making institutions of higher learning more gender inclusive. Unfortunately, the number of women accessing university education through this strategy remains a drop in the ocean – metaphorically speaking. What are needed urgently are creative and pro-active ways of addressing gender disparities from lower levels of education.

Firstly, existing evidence of the relatively high private and social returns to investments in women and girls has been indisputable. Secondly, in the light of existing evidence, it would be illogical for any government not to invest in women's higher education as key in human capital development. Hence, reason dictates that general policy interventions may not be adequate in ensuring gender parity in higher education or even enhancing investment in human capital unless they target girls and women specifically, outside and within community and family settings. This sort of targeting is justifiable for two reasons, the first one being that women are disproportionately represented among the poor, unemployed and uneducated. Hence, targeting girls and women could be an effective strategy for reducing poverty and consequently being able to eradicate other factors that have continued to hamper development of female human capital through a relegation of women to low-level education and training. Secondly, we need to accept that the mission of universities is not a charitable one but a commercial one. Hence, increased female enrolment in such institutions has little to do with ensuring gender parity and more to do with tapping the wealth of rich families whose children could not qualify for public universities, and many of who happen to be girls. Short of affirmative action and providing scholarships or bursaries to girls, no institution of higher learning can claim to address gender inequities that negatively affect the education of women and girls (see World Bank 1995:10-11).

While superficially gender equity is about numbers and representation of women and men in public life and in education, it is important to take cognizance of the fact that equity per se cannot be a panacea to the deep-rooted causes of social inequality, including gender inequality. Access to educational opportunities at the primary level and the secondary sector, relies on a combination of factors, with gender being key. Central to this concern is the legacy of neglect by discriminatory historical systems that created problems that are likely to persist for a long while. Hence, national governments need to develop appropriate policy frameworks that would guide transformation within educational systems.

Diversity of academic programmes as an indicator of equity

It has been pointed out elsewhere in this study that the type of programmes offered in universities should include an equity component. This is not only in terms of giving students an equal chance of joining academic programmes of their choice, but that universities design programmes that contribute to human capital development in areas that society most needs skills. Put it another way, the broadening of access to higher education institutions should be concentrated in areas that will benefit most members of society in terms of professional skills utilisation. In Kenya, the *Report of the Presidential working party for the establishment of tne second university* had identified such areas to be industrial technology, agricultural engineering, veterinary and human medicine, and forestry, with aspects of sociology integrated in all this areas. What this meant was that any future expansion of higher education would be along these lines if skills from higher education were to be equitably distributed among the Kenyan population. The question that this study sought to address in this respect is the extent to which the privatisation of higher education has contributed to human capital development in such key areas.

For purposes of comparison, Table 3.5 is a summary of competitive degree courses in public universities – courses that most students apply for but that the universities do not have adequate space to admit all the applicants. These are the areas that the Kenyan population requires skilled personnel, especially to move qualified professional people from the urban to the rural areas.

Public universities offer a total of 178 degree programmes, out of which less than 30 are rated highly with regard to their responsiveness to social needs. If the imperative for privatisation was to fill gaps in terms of unmet demand, to what extent have private universities and programmes met these expectations? In Table 3.6, a summary of the major undergraduate programmes in private universities is given.

Private universities have focussed on offering courses that require less financial investment to establish. Most of the private universities therefore have avoided critical programmes such as Medicine and Engineering. These subjects had been identified to constitute areas where the country lacked a skilled work force. Unmet demand in some of these technical areas is partly what fuelled the need to expand higher education through privatisation.

Table 3.5: Competitive degree programmes in Kenya public universities

Institution	Programmes
University of Nairobi	1. Bachelor of Science (Agricultural Engineering) 2. Bachelor of Commerce 3. Bachelor of Science (Civil Engineering) 4. Bachelor of Science (Electrical Engineering) 5. Bachelor of Science (Mechanical Engineering) 6. Bachelor of Law 7. Bachelor of Dental Surgery (B.D.S) 8. Bachelor of Pharmacy 9. Bachelor of Medicine and Bachelor of Surgery 10. Bachelor of Science (Nursing) 11. Bachelor of Science (Actuarial Science) 12. Bachelor of Science (Computer Science)
Kenyatta University	1. Bachelor of Commerce 2. Bachelor of Science (Computer Science) 3. Bachelor of Science (Telecommunication and Information technology) 4. Bachelor of Science (Computer Engineering) 5. Bachelor of Science (Software Engineering) 6. Bachelor of Education (Science) 7. Bachelor of Education Special Education and Early Childhood Education)
Jomo Kenyatta University	1. Bachelor of Science (Biochemical and Processing Engineering) 2. Bachelor of Science (Electrical and Electronic Engineering) 3. Bachelor of Science (Mechatronics Engineering)
Moi University	1. Bachelor of Technology (Production Engineering) 2. Bachelor of Technology (Electrical and Communication Engineering) 3. Bachelor of Medicine and Bachelor of Surgery 4. Bachelor of Technology (Chemical and Process Engineering) 5. Bachelor of Science (nursing) 6. Bachelor of Technology (Computer Engineering)

The high entry costs into engineering and technology-based courses seem to keep private universities from venturing into these academic fields. It is also true that, at the time when most of the private universities were accredited, about 82 percent of Kenyan students who went to higher education in India were in either Commerce or Arts 'soft' degree programmes (Deloitte and Touche 1994). However, this was more of a second choice alternative as competitive courses such as medicine and engineering are not easily open to foreign students who go for higher education in India.

Table 3.6: Key degree programmes in private universities in Kenya

Institution	Programmes
Daystar University	Bachelor of Arts and Religious Studies, Communication, Community Development, Music, Psychology
	Bachelor of Commerce
	Bachelor of Education
	Bachelor of Science (Economics)
USIU	Bachelor of Arts (International Relations)
	Bachelor of Arts (Journalism)
	Bachelor of Arts (Psychology)
	Bachelor of Science (Business Administration, Hotel and Restaurant Management, Information Systems and Technology, International Business Administration and Tourism Management)
CUEA	Bachelor of Education (Arts)
	Bachelor of Education (Science)
	Bachelor of Arts
	Bachelor of Laws
	Commerce
UEAB	Bachelor of business Administration
	Bachelor of Education
	Bachelor of Arts
	Bachelor of Science and Technology
	Public Health

Source: Field data.

The conclusion here is that private universities have been able to respond to skills in two areas. One is commerce and business administration. In the 2004–2005 academic year for example, USIU registered 1800 undergraduates in this programme. Strathmore had 550 undergraduates registered in the same programme. By comparison, the University of Nairobi registered 2514 undergraduates for the same programme. The other programme is MBA where USIU registered 300 while Nairobi had 1364 students. Private universities do not offer other professional courses such as engineering, computer science, medicine and law. The University of Nairobi that offers the programmes only manages to register 30 percent of the students. This leaves a huge unmet demand that the private universities are not responding to, due to a lack of programme diversification. Private universities have also concentrated on offering vocational subjects that were previously offered at middle level colleges. Because of this situation, a good percentage of students in private universities are in non-degree programmes. This raises two critical issues related to private higher education and national development. One is whether the private universities have added any value to the vocational programmes they offer different from what the middle level colleges used to do. This implies that their contribution to an equitable distribution of highly needed professional skills among the Kenyan population has been negligible. The second relates to need to have a large private university sector that has most of its students in non-degree programmes in a country where qualified students for degree level education often miss out on places in universities. As the private universities indicated, they keep applicants on the waiting list for some time before admission is granted, sometimes due to lack of space.

Admission of students with disabilities

According to UNESCO (1998) with regard to the provision for students with disabilities in higher education, the extent of affirmative action for disabled students should include admission policies and institutional support and services. This provision recognises the fundamental role of higher education in the promotion of human rights and democracy. It should therefore be accessible to all on an equitable basis. Some higher education institutions all over the world in recognition of the special circumstances of disabled students and the need to promote equity have certain provisions to increase access and the completion rates of such students. Such provisions include.

- Modified entrance criteria and preferential treatment in choice of subjects;
- Modified entrance criteria that entail a lower examination score threshold for admission or exemption from certain courses;
- Preferential treatment in which students with disabilities are assigned to a department of their first choice provided they meet the minimum requirements.

The access of students with disabilities to higher education may be limited by the lack of adequate and appropriately adaptive facilities to support learning. Of course, depending on the type of disability, such students need different provisions that may require more financial input from the institutions. Students with motor impairment may not for example need as much compared to those with visual, learning, medical or psychological impairment. Since these provisions have cost implications, it is important to establish if private higher education institutions have policies to cater for such students.

The four private universities studied do not have provisions for disabled students in terms of academic programmes and extra-curricular activities. The institutions admit students with minor motor impairment but not on any special scheme, as they are considered 'normal' enough to participate in the activities of the institutions. While some private universities boast of having an edge in the use of information and communication technology, they have not considered using such systems to benefit the hearing and visually impaired students who aspire to higher education. Deliberate policies for admission of disabled students are therefore non-existent in private universities. Among public universities, only Kenyatta University has a policy of admitting disabled students to both public and private programmes. The university also runs a special education programme that trains teachers for students with various disabilities. However, the students do not qualify for government sponsorship and this has tended to limit their numbers.

Conclusions

This section has analysed the dynamics of access and equity to private universities and programmes in Kenya. Access polices related to the operation and mission of the universities, the socioeconomic background of students, gender considerations and admission of students with disabilities have been examined. Data gathered show that the private higher education sector operates in a manner that exacerbates social inequities. In the short-term, the sector places a premium on fee payment, which is priced above the incomes of most Kenyans. This is because of two reasons; one since private universities and programmes in public universities have been established for commercial reasons, the ability to pay tuition fees takes first place over everything else. This situation obtains even for religious institutions that have been established as 'not-for-profit'. Second, there has not been a significant change in the paradigm within which private higher education institutions had been established. Hence, they have continued the process of providing higher education to an elitist class that can afford their charges. In doing so, no fundamental innovations have been made in terms of initial access, admission requirements, gender, diversity of programmes and admission of students with disabilities to ensure that social classes that were left out of the public higher education system have a chance. The only exception is in the admission of continuing and working students. However, this is because the working students can afford payment of fees. This way private higher education has provided more alternatives to social groups that have always enjoyed it.

Private universities did point out that their extent of innovation to accommodate students with various disabilities is limited. Respondents argued that they receive students from systems that are already inequitable from primary and secondary level. However, as Article 3(b) of the World Conference on Higher Education, 1998, states:

> Equity of access to higher education should begin with the reinforcement, and if need be, the reordering of its links with all other levels of education, particularly with secondary education. Higher education institutions must be viewed, and must work within themselves, to be a part of and encourage, a seamless system starting with early childhood and primary education and continuing through life. Higher education institutions must work in active partnerships with parents, schools, students, socio-economic groups and communities. However, access to higher education should remain open to those successfully completing secondary school (UNESCO, Declaration on Higher Education, Article 3(b) 1998 Paris).

None of the private universities and programs in Kenya has taken up the above challenge. The other issue that we pointed out as an indicator on equity is that of quality. In the next section, one aspect of quality is analysed. This is related to the involvement of private higher education in research and knowledge generation.

4

Research and Knowledge Production in Private Universities and Programmes in Kenya

Introduction

The quality of research is one facet of university institutions used to assess their efficiency and effectiveness. The other facets are teaching and public service. The mission of universities is to generate and expand knowledge through research and teaching. This implies that universities should do as much research as teaching and be able to generate financial resources from research grants much as they do from teaching through tuition fees. It has been noted elsewhere in this study that because of their long history with higher education and strong economies, developed countries have differentiated institutions. Some of these institutions focus on research alone, others on teaching while others combine these functions. This option is not tenable in Africa given the small number of institutions, the lack of a vibrant indigenous capital to finance private research universities, and the economic problems facing most of these countries. The university institutions that exist therefore have to combine these services. As argued in Section Three, the quality of universities is an important component of achieving equity. In this chapter, issues on how privatisation and private higher education have affected the mission of the university in terms of research, knowledge production and dissemination in Kenya are discussed.

The research, knowledge production and dissemination mission of universities

From their establishment in the medieval period, universities were bestowed with three interrelated functions; that is research, teaching and public service. During the medieval era, universities were celebrated as sites of intellectual discovery and excitement, places for adventure and discovery of new ideas and theories (Ross 1976). The university communities (students and professors) were united by and devoted to knowledge and learning. The will to seek without limitation, and allow reason to blossom and establish truths that were disseminated to succeeding generations through various mechanisms, such as publications and seminars were central to the functioning of universities.

The idea of the university, at least in a classical sense, incorporated the tenets of the need to pursue research. University research was distinguished by three traditions from other forms of research. The first tradition was that such research had to be based on cumulative scholarship. This form of research differed from inspirational or intuitive research which in the words of Nisbet:

> ...does not disparage reason, intuition or common sense. Like the first, it aims at wisdom, truth, enlightenment ... But differs from the first in the monumental emphasis that is placed on cumulative knowledge, corporate knowledge that is gained by man working in terms of the works of others; the kind of knowledge that declares the indispensability of profound learning regarding what others have said about these texts, sources and words (Nisbet 1971:31).

The above view stressed the traditional role of the university in seeking knowledge for knowledge's sake, and an emphasis on basic as opposed to applied or contract research. The aim was to build systematic knowledge required for insight and understanding. The second tradition that guided classical university research was that it had to be carried out without regard to utilitarian application or potential social gain. In other words, the search for truth was not to be influenced or directed by social needs or anticipation of material gains. A researcher's work was directed solely by his/her inner curiosity and desire to know. The last tradition was that research time and interests were to be balanced by the professors' obligation to teaching.

This classical understanding of the research mission of universities still obtains to some degree. However, certain modifications, in terms of understandings, expectations and obligations have occurred. The impetus for such changes include, but are not limited to, post-war developments at the international level, paradigm changes in the social sciences that have been occasioned by the post-Cold War ideological realignments and economic austerity in developing countries. These issues continue to determine the degree and speed of the growth of private higher education in most of Africa and their capacity to engage in research.

Post-war developments and research in universities

A discussion of post-war development in terms of the research mission of universities is important here. In developing countries, including Kenya, universities are not indigenous institutions. They were transplanted to these countries by the colonial powers at the end of formal colonialism. The university models found in former colonised countries reflect the structure of universities of the colonial powers at the time. Second, certain post-war developments influenced the re-conceptualisation of the research mission of the universities, which perceptions were also transplanted to the colonies. Among the developments were the reconstruction needs of post-war societies that required new applications of knowledge and technology, the need for new systems of social engineering to avoid the possibility of another war, and the worldwide demand for the expansion of the higher education system.

Due to the above imperatives, arguments were made regarding the fact that the classical medieval university was isolated from society in its research function. It was also argued that research for knowledge, as an end in itself, should be amalgamated with a redefined mission of a university as a problem solving research institution. Henceforth, a university had to be evaluated as a producer, wholesaler and retailer of knowledge (Ross 1976).

Within the western colonial countries, the success of universities started to be measured in terms of providing advanced education, fostering research and scientific development and assisting their societies in the task of development (Altbach 1992). The use of higher education research findings was encouraged. Furthermore, universities became the citadels of knowledge networks that included research institutions and the means of knowledge dissemination such as journals and publishing houses. This was the idea of the university and its research function that was transferred to African countries at independence.

In terms of methodology and research protocols, most research in African universities was influenced by and depended on received western methodological and theoretical orientations, produced in western universities through programmes that claimed to build 'capacity' and 'indigenous knowledge' systems. Western countries continued to have a hold on the direction of research in African countries. Up to the 1980s, Western governments through organisations such as the Rockefeller and Ford Foundations gave scholarships to African students to train in Western universities. The claims of the programmes were to build local research capacity that would be instrumental in addressing African developmental problems. The training, ideas and research methods were largely western. This became the genesis of the internationalisation of social science methodologies. In a sense, this created an international knowledge system that helped to circulate ideas and maintain the research hegemony of the western university culture in African universities and scholarship (Altbach 1992).

The knowledge and institutional problems that were transferred have largely marginalised relevant research in African countries. By the 1990s, therefore, the claim of African universities to be engaging in relevant research, and disseminating the same, was suspect. Perhaps this is why there has been a continuous contention that African universities have contributed little in terms of research relevant to the development of their countries. The question that therefore continues to occupy African governments and policy makers, is 'how can higher education and its research contribute to play a more active role in the elimination of poverty, hunger, disease, ignorance, over-production of quality graduates?' (Ajayi et al., 1996). The other issue is to examine how the commercial logic of private higher education fits into this logic. Universities in Africa, whether private or public, face two challenges in this regard. The first is to focus their mission on solving the problems of the societies where they are located. The second is to remain relevant to the global forces that drive higher education as an international institution. The logic of private higher education both in terms of its structures and in terms of functions fits more into the international frame than into the needs arising from specific country conditions. In any event, the growth of private higher education in Africa has been triggered more by global forces than any national planning. This reality may affect the extent to which private higher education invests in research that addresses local problems or engages in any research at all.

Ideological and paradigmatic changes in the social sciences

The central logic upon which research is carried out and solutions implemented has shifted. What is identified as a problem for research and the methodologies used to study it are subject to the dictates of certain ideological orientations. Such orientations are fashioned by the realities of power that lie with those who control the knowledge protocols and wider political economy structures that influence financial allocations. University research in Africa has for long been based on social science methodologies that were influenced by the enlightenment project of modernity. Three characteristics marked this modernity project. First was that the theories and methodologies were Euro-centric, though African researchers heavily relied on them. Second, the enlightenment project, as propounded by classical theorists, was based on a claim to a neutral value free and objective social science. Third, most of the theories that were used to research third world development issues were based on this modernity project. However, the fact that decades of the application of these theories did not help bring about development in the Third World, as in western Europe, cast doubt on their scientific objectivity. In particular, neo-liberalism has argued that the modernity research project that emphasised reason, science, progress and universal knowledge was obsolete. The neo-liberals represent an ideological sift in research protocols. The research focus of the neo-liberal paradigm is on different and culturally specific theories and categories as the new basis upon which research has to be based.

In brief, neo-liberalism by discarding the liberal enlightenment project has shifted the basis of research from purely positivist protocols to various forms of relativism, but claim to be objective by giving space to individual voices, and paying attention to local realities. Of course, there is still the contested assumption that the local, the individual voice, is not influenced by an external force. It is important to note here that private higher education focuses on the interests of individual students as clients, not as members of a large collectivity. What is critical here, and as far as this study is concerned, is to examine how a private university sector is interrogating these perspectives to produce relevant research and engage in knowledge dissemination.

Despite the shift in research paradigms, universities remain key institutions to steer the socioeconomic development of their countries through research. As Teferra & Altbach (2003) note, universities remain the most important institutions in the production and consumption of knowledge. In the increasingly global world that is being shaped by knowledge and information, establishing a strong research infrastructure has more than ever before become a sine qua non (Teferra & Altbach 2003:9).They serve as knowledge brokers and training grounds for policy makers and national leaders. They create and provide a portal for the dissemination of new technologies, often acting as lead agents for the economy to absorb computer and telecommunication innovations (ASPEN 1999). For individual universities, the challenge is not to remain stuck in the old research protocols, but to be innovative in their teaching, research and public service functions. They should also be instrumental in building the human resources and stimulating social and economic development in their communities (ASPEN 1999). For the private higher education sector, especially in Africa, investing in research as much as in teaching will reflect a commitment to the development agenda of the continent. In any case, part of the justification for private higher education has been to increase access and provide the knowledge that supposedly the continent lacked in the twentieth century.

The other issue that has had a bearing on research in universities is that of globalisation. Much has been written on the political and economic implications of globalisation. Both privatisation and liberalisation of the public service sectors have been local expressions of the extent to which countries have embraced the tenets of globalisation. The idea of choice and the market in private higher education is closely tied to these processes. This implies the commercialisation of ideas, including research ideas, theoretical postulates and epistemological grounding of research knowledge. Despite these developments, the world is still characterised by inequities, unevenness, social exclusion and polarisation (Griffin & Khan 1992). In the midst of all this change, new economic, social political, cultural and linguistic problems have come up, problems that underlie the prevalence of extreme poverty, unequal gender relations, crime and deviance (Aina 1997). These problems require new rethinking, new ideological orientations, new research methodologies and techniques. Private higher education or higher education in general has to take up these problems in its research.

Universities as research institutions can be counted on to come up with new ideas to confront these crises. Universities in the developing world that do not exploit the use of electronic libraries, publication of out of print and current books on-line, and free software may stifle the research creativity of their scholars. In a globalising world where the standard and quality of life depend upon the power of knowledge, and socioeconomic development is becoming more and more knowledge-intensive, the role of higher education becomes crucial, especially in research (UNESCO 1993). However, some general observations have been made that African universities do not seem to have a comprehensive plan regarding how they can contribute to the development of their communities through research and consultancy (Ajayi et al., 1996). Many of these deficiencies are not due to a lack of scholarly capacity, but to inadequate research funding. In a privatised environment, it is imperative to document how far this situation has deteriorated, or improved.

The world conference on higher education convened by UNESCO (1998), defined a renewed vision on the mission of higher education. The vision reiterated the role of higher education to advance, create, and disseminate knowledge. This would be achieved through research and provision of service to the community, to assist societies in cultural, social and economic development, promotion and development of scientific and technological research, as well as research in the social sciences, the humanities and creative arts (Article 1(c) 1998). This vision would be achieved through

(a) The advancement of knowledge through research. This can be achieved by higher education systems that promote postgraduate studies. A balance should be established between basic and applied (target, oriented), research.

(b) Higher education institutions should ensure that all members of the academic community engaged in research are provided with appropriate training, resources and support. The intellectual and cultural rights for the results of the research should be used to the benefit of humanity and should not be abused.

(c) Research should be enhanced in all disciplines, including the social and human sciences, education, engineering, natural sciences, mathematics, information technology and the arts, within a framework of national, regional and international research and development policies. Of importance is the enhancement of research capacities in higher education, research institutions, as mutual enhancement of quality takes place when higher education and research are conducted at a high level within the same institution. The financial and material support required should be sourced from both public and private sources.

(d) Relevance in higher education should be assessed in terms of the fit between what society expects of institutions and what they do. This requires ethical standards, political impartiality, critical capacities, and at the same time, a better articulation with the problems of society and the world of work based on long-term orientations on societal aims and needs. (Summarised from Articles 51 b, c and Article 61 of UNESCO 1998).

Economic austerity and research in African universities

The economic crisis of most African countries has also had a bearing on the nature of research in African universities. As has been discussed, up to the 1980s African universities received funds for research and postgraduate training from western countries. Such funding was provided within the broad political economy of Cold War imperatives, and the modernity project of universalising the social science research ethos. The end of the Cold War and the advent of globalisation reduced funding from western countries to African universities for research and postgraduate training. These conditions accelerated Africa's economic crisis with little or no funding for higher education programmes, especially research. As African countries sunk more into debt and underdevelopment, the international development paradigm changed in favour of market economics and liberalisation. This in essence meant the selling out of public enterprises to private interests, most of which happen to be western multinationals. This had direct negative implications for African higher education, research and development agenda. The forces of globalisation and market economies reduced the demand for a high-level work force in the public service and private sector. Due to the lack of research and investment in high capital academic programmes in the universities, critical unemployment of university graduates has been accompanied with severe shortage of a skilled work force in science and technology-based areas (Ajayi et al. 1996).

The pre-privatisation period saw, to some degree, indigenous public enterprises emerging and creating a demand for relevant research in public universities. Indeed, in the case of Kenya, this study established that before the economic crisis of the 1990s, universities responded well to this mission. However, the post-1990 marketisation saw this agenda taken over by private interests, those that were able to fund research agendas, and this led to the growth of the consultancy industry outside universities.

Further, and this observation was important to this study, the decrease in research funds has led to calls for universities to establish linkages with industry. The assumptions here have been that such linkages can create an altruistic working relationship between the universities and industry where industry will fund research and the universities will produce the knowledge to benefit the industry's commercial interests. However, what is most overlooked in this line of thinking is that Kenya does not have an indigenous industrial sector. Like most developing countries, what exists in Kenya are industrial extensions of multinational corporations, and more often, basic research that aids the operation of such industries is done in their countries of origin. Of course, they engage in on the job research and training for their staff to boost productivity, but this is often small scale, and limited to applied research and does not lead to discovery of any new knowledge relevant to the socioeconomic needs of the majority of Kenyans.

The neglect of basic scientific research in universities has been accentuated by the market fundamentalism principles within which private higher education operates. Such principles have influenced universities to look at 'good' knowledge as something that guarantees university graduates jobs, or perfects their skills in doing existing jobs, not something that leads to innovation and new scientific discoveries. While admitting that their university does not engage in much research, the Vice-Chancellor of USIU noted that seventy percent of graduates from the university obtained employment or settled into private business within six months of graduation (*East African Standard*, 30 November 2005). However, and as historical evidence shows, countries develop by investing in basic scientific research that gives people new options. The present trend in the privatisation and marketisation of higher education has skewed universities to engage in applied research that only meet the 'market' needs of western industry while ignoring the development needs of developing societies

As the World Bank's (1987) report sadly attests, research in African universities collapsed in the 1980s due to the financial crisis. Good quality postgraduate training also declined. This situation jeopardises Africa's long-run ability to take advantage of the worldwide advance in science and technology (World Bank 1987:73). African countries need to increase their capacity to absorb and use new knowledge through the development of indigenous postgraduate teaching and research programmes. Indeed, it is only through this engagement that countries can participate in the global knowledge economy as equal partners.

Level of research and postgraduate training in private universities and in programmes of public universities

Has the privatisation and marketisation of university programmes encompassed a research agenda? Field data for the study from the private programmes of public universities and purely private universities showed a mixed and inconclusive picture. For public universities, there is no system of keeping track of the research assignments of faculty members. The number of faculty members engaged in research is difficult to establish, as universities do not have a centralised system where such information is reported. The repeated responses from both public and private universities was that 'very few' lecturers are engaged in any research. The regular schedule of most lecturers in public universities is divided into three: teaching regular students, teaching private students in public universities, and teaching part-time students in private universities. In this regard, it is important to point out that most private universities engage about 60 percent of their staff as part-time personnel from public universities. Besides, the rigours of writing and applying for research grants have made teaching a quicker option to make money.

Universities also encouraged the above trends by pegging the amount of money paid out for teaching private students to the number of hours and students taught. The effect of this proviso has been that most lecturers have been unable to qualify for promotion due to a lack of research experience and publications. Most of the teaching staff stagnates at the lecturer rank for a long time. Statistics compiled by this study from records held by CHE indicated that as of 2003, some 3.7 percent of the teaching staff in public and private universities was at the rank of professor, 7.2 percent as associate professors, 21 percent as senior lecturers, 51 percent as lecturers, and 18 percent as assistant lecturers. Comparisons between public and private universities are of course more revealing. The University of Nairobi had 4.2 percent of its staff as full professors against 52 percent of lecturers. At Moi University, the figure was 2.6 percent against 66 percent. Kenyatta University had 4.4 percent against 44 percent, while Jomo Kenyatta had one percent professorial staff compared to 53 percent as lecturers. At the private universities, UEAB had 4.5 percent full professors and 54 percent lecturers. CUEA had one percent full professors against 27 percent lecturers and 49 percent assistant lecturers. Daystar had 46 percent lecturers against 3.6 percent associate professors. USIU had a different distribution, with 13 percent full professors, 40 percent senior lecturers, and 21 percent lecturers. It should however be pointed out, but not to a point of generalisation, that most professors in private universities migrated from public universities after failing to meet research and publication conditions for promotion.

The encouragement of teaching and more teaching has distracted lecturers from balancing their obligations for teaching, research and community service. To the universities, this may be seen as a short-term financial saving. Having most staff at lecturer level translates into less financial allocation for salaries, as lecturers are not highly paid. These are tentative indicators that privatisation has been a bane for research and knowledge production both in public and private universities. The involvement of lecturers from public and private universities in research that is not reflected in the academic activities of the universities reinforces Mkandawire's (1998) observations. The privatisation era has been accompanied by the growth of the consultancy industry that does not reflect the movement towards a more knowledge-intensive development strategy by national governments but a growing incapacitation, and even marginalisation of the African states, and the preponderance of donor interests.

An analysis of the volume of budgets that universities vote for and actually expend for research can provide an indication of institutional commitment to this course. Even during the pre-privatisation days, budgets for research in public universities had been substantially reduced. One of the arguments for privatisation was that private sector participation could provide the much-needed money for research. However, the market logic of private higher education lays a focus on short-term intensive training while most research at least in its basic orientation is a long-term process. Relevant training, especially on the job, in the form of executive undergraduate and postgraduate programmes is now the norm in most private education institutions. Such programmes do not give an adequate academic grounding for a research oriented scholarly community. Comparing budgets for research, the forms of research and the participants of such can unravel the direction of research under a privatised higher education system.

Among the private universities, CUEA provides the most elaborate research agenda complete with a research committee and funds voted for the purpose. The university has a Department of Research that coordinates the evaluation of research proposals from faculty, awards research funds and peer reviews research reports for publication. The mission statement of the department is stated as 'the undertaking of independent and collaborative research work across departments of the university in order to inform social and economic policy and monitor implementation of programmes'. The extent to which the university's research work links to policy is however not stated. There was evidence also that research agendas largely reflect the religious orientation of the university. The mandate of the research committee entailed the following:

- The promotion and coordination of relevant scientific research in the faculties and departments of the university;
- The promotion of collaboration between CUEA and Catholic institutions involved in higher education;
- The organisation and coordination of inter-faculty staff seminars;

- The promotion of research collaboration with other universities and higher education institutions;
- Collaboration between faculty and the faculty research committee of the university in matters of research;
- Assessment and approval of research proposals submitted for funding;
- Maintenance of a register of approved research proposals.

The university operates and allocates research grants into different categories.

(a) Faculty research grants, which are meant to help faculty conduct research on a topic of interest. Five research grants are offered each year on a competitive basis. The amount for each grant does not exceed Ksh 150,000 (US$ 2,000).
(b) Faculty research grants for graduate study include five awards each year for faculty members who are doctoral degree students. The amount of this grant does not exceed Ksh 150,000 (US$ 2,000) per year.
(c) A Departmental research project fund is targeted at support for departmental projects. The amount voted for each department per year does not exceed Ksh 100,000 (US$ 1,333).
(d) A research capacity building fund is earmarked to be used by CUEA staff to organise short courses on research. The amount available under the vote did is limited to Ksh 100,000 (US$ 1,333) per year.
(e) Project and activities grants are awarded each year for innovative projects addressing the situation of the underprivileged. The amount of the grant is limited to Ksh 200,000 (US$ 2,666) per year.

At USIU, the largest secular private university, there was no evidence of allocation of funds for research and development. The university had no allocation for research or public functions for the academic years 1999–2000 to 2004–2005.

At the other private universities, claims of accomplished or ongoing research could not be confirmed. It is possible that some of these were individual consultancies by the few members of staff who were on permanent employment. The view of research at the institutions was linked to their missions as Christian institutions. The mission statements of the institutions show a commitment to revealed knowledge. All the universities stress the belief that knowledge comes from God, and should be used for purposes of building faithful Christian communities. At Daystar University, for example, the purpose of their research programme is stated as to 'understand the various people and groups in Africa in order to develop effective means of communicating the gospel'. Examples that were given of the university's research programme were studies on

- The un-reached peoples in Kenya;
- The Nairobi church survey;
- The Kenya Youth survey.

The university's research programme is offered at the level of a two-year diploma in 'Research and consultation'. The university also has an institute of Christian ministries and training (ICMT), which provides short-term training on 'Research and Consultancy'.

Generally, the four private universities have not taken up research as a core component of their programmes. The other private universities that are not covered in this study, but which were reviewed briefly in Section Two, are still establishing themselves. The only larger secular university, USIU, indicated after establishing as a teaching university, integrating research into their programmes was the next agenda. Private higher education in Kenya has therefore had much more focus on teaching than research.

The issue of research and knowledge production in private higher education institutions that are being established in many developing countries is critical. Elsewhere in this study the point has been made that given the demand and the size of the university sector in Kenya, institutions have to combine the teaching function, the development of new knowledge function, and the provision of services to society function. There are always claims that private higher education should focus on absorbing demand and teaching only those skills that the economy demands, as these have been the imperatives driving the growth of the sector. Investing in research would however deepen the relevance of private higher education institutions. Progress in the era of globalisation and privatisation depends on the knowledge economy, and universities are critical as generators and disseminators of new knowledge. Focussing on research will therefore enhance the relevance of private higher education to the 'marketisation' process and the development needs of societies where they are located. The globalisation era that has spurred the growth of private universities sees research not as an option but an important imperative of higher education institutions.

The public universities present diverse situations. The opening up of public universities to private students was meant to generate extra income for the universities to utilise in shoring up their defences against deteriorating standards. Part of this revenue, it was thought, would be voted for research. More of the funds generated however have ended up being utilised in other areas not related to the universities' core mission. At the University of Nairobi for example only one percent of the funds generated from the private programmes from during the period from 1997 to 2002 was allocated to research (Kiamba 2003:11). This sum can be compared to the 41 percent, 10 percent and 9 percent that was allocated to salaries, capital development and utilities respectively. The other universities have developed a system where 5 percent of the income generated is voted for research. This does not however translate into much money given the size of the universities and the fact that some academic areas, especially medicine and the sciences, require large capital outlays. For example at Kenyatta University, about Ksh 3 million (US$ 40,000) was voted for research in the 2003–2004 academic years. Once distributed each of the six schools of the university received an average of Ksh 500,000 (US$ 6,666) to distribute among faculty members for research. This money would not accomplish much.

Public universities however receive money from the government and donors for research. In the 2004–2005 period, the government allocated Ksh 700 million (US$ 933,333) to be distributed to the universities for research by the National Council of Science and Technology. Public universities also access donor funds for research through collaborative arrangements. The University of Nairobi's medical school was for example involved in a collaborative research project on a vaccine for AIDS with John Hopkins medical school. The research spearheaded by the International AIDS Vaccine Initiative (IAVI) and the Kenya AIDS Vaccine Initiative (KAVI), however got entangled in problems of rights to patents that accompanied the funding. At Kenyatta University, lecturers from the School of Environmental Sciences were involved in research related to the organic growing of maize. The collaborating agency was the International Centre for Research on Agriculture and Forestry (ICRAF). There are also regional bodies that award research funds on a competitive basis. Some of these institutions are the inter-university Council of East Africa (IUCEA), located in Uganda and the Institute for Capacity Building and Development (AICAD) located in Kenya and housed in the compound of the Jomo Kenyatta University of Science and Technology. Pan-African institutions such as OSSREA and CODESRIA have also always provided research grants to budding scholars.

The research grants from regional and pan-African institutions are not restricted to the public universities. The number of faculty from private universities who enter these competitions successfully is however small. Even in public universities, research grants revolve around a few lecturers who regularly enter the competitions. As earlier mentioned, the choice is between teaching and leaning towards research. Public universities, because of their long history and large faculty, have lecturers who desire to concentrate on research and others who want to teach. In the private universities, given their relatively short history, a research tradition has not taken root. Besides, private universities initially attracted lecturers who wanted to make more money through part-time teaching. These lecturers still account for a higher percentage of the faculty in these universities. A research focus and tradition has therefore yet to emerge in the private university institutions.

Public universities however have another advantage in terms of accessing research funds. Most donor funds for research target strengthening the capacity of public sector institutions where the universities fall. Besides having the human resources for research therefore, this latter factor gives them an edge over private universities.

Besides the availability of funds, the research culture of universities is nurtured through relevant postgraduate teaching and research. The study sought to establish what implications the privatising of public universities and the development of private higher education had had on this aspect. Postgraduate training is important in terms of building a future cohort of researchers who will take over from old and retiring faculty members. The number of postgraduate students who enrol and graduate, especially at PhD level, on research-based courses, is therefore an important indicator of institutional commitment to research.

A noticeable trend in private higher education institutions is the enrolment of postgraduate students in a few specific programmes that have been defined as 'marketable' and offered through course work. This means that courses that enable students to get job placements as soon as possible are emphasised. Topping the list of these courses are Bachelor of Commerce and Masters of Business administration (MBA) options. At USIU, these options generate the bulky of the university's operating revenues as they enrol about 85 percent of the total student population. At CUEA, most students enrol for business studies, accounting, business administration, marketing and management of resources and finance. According to the university registrar, the demand for these courses is so high that students who did not meet the requirements were willing to enrol for bridging courses. The registrar noted that 'high school leavers walk into my office and say they want to study B.Com. When I ask what they want to specialise in, they are lost for words' (Registrar, CUEA, quoted in the *East African Standard*, 8 April 2004:7).

A high concentration of postgraduate training in both the private and public universities is at the masters level. A majority of these students are driven by the desire for career mobility with an added masters degree, and do not aim at pursuing an academic career. This is not to imply that systems of postgraduate training should be tailored to produce career academicians. Any system should have the capacity to rejuvenate itself in a sustainable manner. Academicians deal with knowledge production through research and institutions should factor training in such areas as core to their functioning. Besides, the whole idea of providing diversity should be viewed from both a structural and functional perspective. Structurally in terms of curricula that cater for diverse interests and functionally in terms of producing graduates who fit varied societal expectations. Postgraduate training, even in a privatised higher education system, should strike a balance between the immediate concern of individual students and the market and long-term training needs of the academic community.

The craze to register for masters degree courses for the purpose of career mobility affects the disciplines of business education, commerce, law, and education. At Kenyatta University, in the School of Education for example, about 90 percent of privately sponsored postgraduate students (masters level) are registered in the Department of Educational Administration and Planning. Most of the students are serving teachers who view an added degree in Educational Administration as a gateway from the classroom to central administration in the hierarchy of the Ministry of Education (personal communication, with M. Ed. students). However, fewer and fewer of these students reapply to come back for higher academic degrees. The story is the same at the University of Nairobi. During the 2004–2005 academic year, there were only 43 students enrolled for the Bachelor of Science, mathematics, course compared to about 300 in psychology. The faculty of law was most popular with 1,000 undergraduate students, but this popularity was not matched at postgraduate level where only 33 students had registered for masters degrees. The reason given for this was that 'lawyers still make money even without higher degrees' (personal communication with law degree students). This perception affects most of the competitive degree course offered by the university such as commerce, medicine and all engineering courses. This means that the privatisation and liberalisation of higher education has made universities lose their role as custodians of knowledge, except where that knowledge is related to some economic gain.

Postgraduate education at most of the private universities is limited to the level of masters degrees. CUEA however has a few students registered for PhD degrees. Both USIU and CUEA also indicated they had given scholarships to some faculty members to go overseas for PhD training. The number of lecturers could however not be ascertained. The slow development of PhD level training for staff development in private universities is perhaps a cost-saving measure fuelled by reliance on part-time lecturers from public universities. Their capacity for mounting academic and policy research is therefore low. The overriding motivation for launching new academic programmes in the private institutions and programmes were:

(a) The capacity of the programme to generate more money for the institutions;
(b) The capacity of the programme to be self-sustaining such that the institutions would not be obliged to subsidise its operations;
(c) The capacity of the programme to attract the highest number of students, sometimes irrespective of entry qualifications; and
(d) The positive evaluation of the programme by the 'market' in terms of how soon graduates could secure employment and attendant remuneration.

Such rigid considerations do not only limit the number of postgraduate students, but also accord less space for any purely academic research to generate knowledge for knowledge's sake. Table 4.0 summarises the number of degrees granted by USIU from 2000–2004. This summary illustrates the absence of PhD-level training. This illustration is important in relaying the situation of the other private universities, since USIU is the largest secular private university.

Table 4.0: Degrees granted by USIU by level, 2000–2004

Years	Total number of degrees	Bachelors	Masters	Doctorate	Others
2000	435	387 (88.97%)	48 (11.03%)	0	0
2001	587	517 (88.07%)	70 (11.93%)	0	0
2002	502	416 (82.87%)	86 (17.13%)	0	0
2003	702	597 (85.04%)	105 (14.96%)	0	0
2004	483	386 (79.92%)	97 (20.08%)	0	0

Source: USIU Data Element Report, 2005

The conclusion that can be deduced from this discussion is that private universities and programmes attract many more undergraduate than postgraduate students. Postgraduate programmes are concentrated at the level of masters degrees, and in a few areas that in the perception of students enhance their chances for employability and job mobility.

Lastly we can refer to courses in research methodology. From the outset, it should be pointed out that there is growing public opinion in Kenya to the effect that privatisation has distorted and subverted the research mission of higher education (see the *East African Standard*, Blackboard section, 18 February and 30 November 2005 issues). Views are expressed that private higher education has lowered the standards of education and that a good research agenda and the relevance of academic programmes are still hostages of inadequate funding, that universities are generally resistant to reforms, and their mission has been compromised by too much teaching and no research. This mission entails the search for truth and generation of new knowledge without undue influence by the need for commercial application or external justification. It also includes the preservation and transmission of this knowledge. In contrast, the norms of private business practices negate the established traditions of the academic profession that require professional autonomy in matters of research, and a less materialist culture.

An analysis of the teaching programmes of the four private universities revealed a lack of specific programmes for teaching research methods, issues, paradigms and protocols. This means that students at the institutions do not enjoy any critical exposure on how to conduct field studies in the social or physical sciences. Postgraduate programmes at the institutions are also not well developed in terms of course contents and student numbers. The most developed postgraduate degree in the private universities is the 'executive' Master of Business Administration (MBA). The research component of the programme utilises applied research protocols limited to library desk reviews, and therefore inadequate to generate critical basic knowledge.

In the private programmes of public universities, courses on research methodology are offered in the relevant disciplines. However, there is a persistent strong feeling among students that the courses are not given adequate depth to enable students to conduct independent fieldwork research. Whereas in the pre-privatisation days, postgraduate degrees at masters level were offered through course work, examinations and thesis, this has changed to course work, examination and 'project' in most departments that have high student enrolments. The thesis component of the masters degree gave the students a chance to try their hand at independent fieldwork research, of course under the guidance of a senior scholar. The masters by 'project' degree option does not expose a student to any fieldwork experience at all. The implication here is that universities are now registering students for PhD studies who have not had an adequate grounding in fieldwork. This becomes a concern since public universities offer PhD training through supervised fieldwork only. There is no course work component integrated. Since students who register for PhD programmes have not had any experience of conducting fieldwork, universities are contemplating introducing course work on research methodologies for such students. The University of Nairobi had introduced such a component.

The project component of postgraduate degrees is often limited to library research. The usage of the word 'research' has come to connote not a serious collection and interpretation of raw data to generate knowledge, but a desk review of academic works already done, which may not have been a product of any fieldwork. The numbers of students opting for the 'project' alternative are always more than those who endeavour to undertake fieldwork and write a thesis. For example in the 2003–2004 academic year, out of a class of 4,000 students in the faculty of commerce at the University of Nairobi, 1,600 were undertaking MBA degrees through project work (field data). In the faculty of education, of the 8,000 students studying education and liberal arts, 450 of them were undertaking M.Ed and MA (Education) under the project option. At Kenyatta University, in the Department of Educational Administration, the largest department of the school, about 286 students were registered for Masters Courses between 2002 and 2004. Only 41 of these students had indicated any intention of undertaking fieldwork for their programme by thesis, while the rest opted for the project arrangement (field data).

The field data reported above reveal curious trends. In private higher education institutions, not much critical reflection is given to the teaching of research methodologies. Most students are not interested in education for its own sake. This tends to the utilisation of applied research paradigms, thereby subverting the generation of critical basic knowledge. The Christian orientation of the private universities also seems to discourage critical fieldwork methodologies. In the private programmes offered at public universities, students are encouraged to register and complete quickly in order to make room for another cohort for the purpose of making more money for the institution. Students for their part do not want to take the fairly long, but critical, road of research by fieldwork and thesis. This results in most students taking the 'project' option that does not demand a firm grounding in objective research protocols.

It has been indicated that research and knowledge production in African universities has been strongly influenced by western social science in terms of methodologies and research protocols. There has however been the consistent demand from the scholarly community for an indigenous African intellectual research methodology. This is considered important as African developmental problems are unique to Africa and require approaches and solutions grounded on African epistemological thinking and responses to such. However, this challenge does not seem to be addressed by private higher education institutions and programmes. The students registered for postgraduate programmes in private institutions also do not want to take the field research option which take time, but short-term projects that can offer them a quick exit and promotion in the job market.

The relevance of research

Research has two major functions for society. In its basic sense (basic research), it generates new principles and knowledge that are the foundations for social transformation. This makes it possible for an enlightened populace who are able to be innovative and create the social and cultural base for development. In the applied sense (applied research), solutions to key problems are discovered and applied to their resolution. In any society, a key balance between basic and applied research is necessary to create a functional continuum between the general knowledge available and the use of such knowledge to advance the cause of human development. African development problems are known. They constellate around poverty, disease, the lack of managerial skills and the lack of a human capital base for science and technology to take off.

Except the private (parallel programmes) in public universities, the other private institutions are non-indigenous, some obtaining their funding from their countries of origin and religious based organisations, to transmit some knowledge about the societies they represent. Even in the case of public universities, there is constant encouragement that they should work with the private sector for research funding. Unfortunately, countries like Kenya do not have a vibrant indigenous private sector that can combine a nationalist vision to finance research for local problem solving.

The issues of relevance of research were central to this research project. In countries where there are partnerships between private universities and industry, the research agenda is likely to be abstracted from the problems of local communities. Those who fund industry may insist that the skills they require for their industries are included in the curriculum. Industries also may finance research that they find important for their immediate application, not for the utilisation of solving the problems of the communities where they are located. The extent to which global interests can benefit from local academicians without commensurate capital returns has been illustrated with the AIDS research that involved IAVI and KAVI at the University of Nairobi. There are also other issues, such as those related to research patents, and the confidentiality of research findings, which may alter the nature of research in privatised higher education environments, as industrial firms are not interested in basic research, but skewed towards applied and profit-making issues. Research issues that have broader public and social relevance may conflict with the needs of private sector financiers. This can undermine the public service mission of the university. In Kenya, as universities are privatising and marketing their courses, they are being encouraged to be sensitive and serve the immediate needs of society, but the private sector that should fund research also has its interests. This may have implications for the organisation of curriculum, the nature and scope of research, and the relationship between society and the university.

As pointed out, there was a paucity of research at the private universities. The research programs at Daystar University target only Christian communication and consultancy. This focus limits its scope to address social problems in a broader context. Within the private university context, only CUEA has a defined programme of research and themes that address both religious and secular social issues. The main thrust of research at CUEA is in the area of enculturation and contemporary social issues. The university also has a proviso for members of the faculty who compete for the various research grants to adhere to a research ethos. This is intended to encourage originality in research and avoid fabrication, falsification and plagiarism. The University identifies priority areas for research. The themes that had been identified for funding during the 2004–2005 academic year were:

- African Christianity and enculturation;
- Indigenous knowledge systems;
- Integrated rural development;
- HIV/AIDS;
- Empowerment of disadvantaged groups and communities;
- Good governance; and
- Human dignity.

The other private universities do not have much focus on research. This is particularly a concern at USIU, as it is a large secular university that has operated in the country over a long period. It is of course possible that faculty members in the institution undertake some research. However, these could be private initiatives not reflected in the academic programmes of the university. The private universities, besides CUEA, do not have any research policies in terms of funding, execution and dissemination.

The public universities, despite privatisation that forced most lecturers to focus on teaching, still boost critical human capital in research. The problem facing public universities is lack of adequate funds for research. The few research projects that were ongoing in the public universities were critical to national and regional development imperatives. Sustaining the research tempo in public universities in the context of privatisation remains a challenge. The percentage of funds allocated for research needs to be raised to reflect the commitment of the institutions to their mission. Privatisation should not transform public universities into purely teaching institutions. The universities should be doing as much research as they are teaching.

Systems of knowledge dissemination and transmission

Knowledge derived from research is supposed to be disseminated to various stakeholders for it to be useful. The stakeholders for university-level research are the government, the financiers (private sector, NGOs, etc.), academic peers, and the local communities served by the university. For this goal to be achieved in substantial manner, it is imperative that:

- Faculty members engage in research on topics and issues relevant to their calling and that of the stakeholders, on a continuous basis. Research also includes the teaching content by faculty members, as it serves as a means of knowledge renewal.
- Faculty members must regularly publish their findings in books and journals of academic repute as a way of sharing knowledge with peers.
- Through seminars, faculty members can summarise such research findings in academic newsletters, newspapers and as abstracts in avenues that have a wider circulation.

- Attendance and presentation of research findings in learned conference and seminars.
- At the university level, there should be various units where faculty members can post and access latest research topics and findings. These include well-stocked libraries linked to the Internet, research bureaus, and research and policy units.

CUEA, among the private universities, has in place systems of knowledge dissemination and transmission. The university publishes a journal, *The Eastern African Journal of Humanities and Sciences*. This journal is dedicated to the scientific research, and is published twice a year by the Department of Research at the university. CUEA also publishes a quarterly newsletter that contains information on the latest research by faculty members, funding, scholarships, conferences, workshops, seminars and general research activities. Such avenues for dissemination of research findings are not common in the other private universities. The universities connect to the community through open days and outreach or community service activities. The activities are however meant to 'market' the programmes of the universities rather than to disseminate any new knowledge.

At the public universities, research and publications have declined considerably with the advent of private students. This reflects the wider problem of funding to support broad based research, journal publications and subscriptions. To qualify for promotion, lecturers have sometimes had to pool finances and other resources to meet the costs of publishing their works. Such investments however only pay back in terms of promotion. Buying and selling of academic materials has considerably declined even among lecturers. A book on Development Studies whose publication had been funded through resource pooling to which one of the lecturers for this research participated had stayed for two years on the office shelves without a single copy sold ,despite advertisements within the universities.

The large numbers of students coming through the private programmes do not translate into a ready market for educational materials that lecturers can invest in. In all the public universities, printing and photocopying bureaus have become a thriving business as students increasingly rely on photocopied notes and book chapters. Noticeably, this photocopying has been extended to thesis and projects by masters degree students. In a private market system, the options that are available to both consumers and providers target the improvement in quality. The development of private higher education in Kenya contradicts this tendency. Systems of knowledge creation and dissemination have been eroded in favour of practices that encourage entry and exit with ease.

The erosion of a research culture has been undermined more by the high need for lecturers occasioned by the establishment of the private universities in an environment where qualified teaching staff were lacking even before privatisation. The movement of staff from public to private universities on promotion without reference to standing in research and publication was one indication of this malaise. The efforts of public universities to stem this exodus, and other considerations through the relaxation of the criteria for academic promotion from one based on research and publication, in favour of more ambiguous ones, have led to the serious decline of scholarly discourse. In Kenyan public universities it is common for the criteria for promotion to change depending on the personalities involved. There are those who have been promoted on merit based on academic work and classroom teaching. These are however few. Most are promoted on grounds of administrative duties not related to academic work. In one of the public universities covered by this study, the assessment marks awarded to administrative experience for the purpose of promotion were higher than those allocated to research and publications.

The criterion for promotion is sometimes never fixed and rationalised. It is negotiated from time to time according to the identity and personality of applicants due for promotion. Moreover, in some bizarre cases, moving from one university to another without any evidence of scholarly work merits promotion. This is common in newly established public universities and all private universities. Hence there are lecturers who became associate professors by moving to one university and then movement to another makes them full professors. These practices demean the quality of academic work, especially research. Senior staff who have been promoted without due regard to their scholarly output are unlikely to inspire this in their students and the young generation of scholars.

Lecturers in Kenya public universities can be categorised into four groups, according to the findings of this study:

(a) Those who are engaged in teaching are the majority and are paid between 35 and 45 percent of the moneys generated from the tuition fees paid by private students;
(b) A small percentage are engaged in consultancy, often in areas not related to strict scholarship and their own academic fields;
(c) An even smaller percentage engages in critical field research and seeks research funds independently from the universities;
(d) Those who have taken full time administrative appointments, such as heads of departments, heads of schools, directors and registrars. Among this category there are those who have rotated from one position to another as if scared to venture into the classroom or university activities that are strictly related to academics.

The above classification is important as it explains the lack of emphasis on research and knowledge dissemination at the universities. Noting that some professors stop doing research and publishing immediately they obtain their final promotion, public universities are now suggesting the hiring of professors on contract with renewal pegged to research output and publication. (Memorandum to the public universities inspection board presented by Prof. G. Magoha, Vice-Chancellor, University of Nairobi, 2005). Some of these developments indicate the extent to which privatisation and private higher education have altered the logic of research and dissemination of knowledge.

The study did establish the availability of digital libraries at both private and public universities. This allowed lecturers and students keen on advancing their scholarly horizons to access the latest journals and research findings online. There was no evidence, however, of journals and research processes by the faculty from the universities covered in this study posted online.

Conclusions

The development of a critical research agenda is one challenge that private higher education institutions have to overcome. Although they have gained prominence as teaching institutions, their relevance would be enhanced if national research priorities were integrated into their programmes. The private higher education sector in Kenya is dominated by religious based institutions that are established locally. The presence of multinationals in the provision of higher education is limited to the AVU and a few other small-scale franchise operations. While this fact may limit the amount of funds at the disposal of private universities to expend on research, it creates room for them to develop a locally relevant research focus, free from multinational interests in the medium term.

The public universities boast of good levels of human capital to deploy for research purposes. Funding has been a problem. The universities have also been operating without a defined research policy. The controversy between the IAVI and KAVI at the University of Nairobi was a consequence of this lack of policy. The intended establishment of a research policy by the University (*East African Standard*, 26 November 2005:1), should be the case in all the other universities.

5

Conclusion: Challenges and Prospects for Private Higher Education in Kenya as regards Equity, Research and Knowledge Production

Introduction

The privatisation of public universities and the entry of private higher education institutions in Kenya constitute critical period in a strategy for the development of higher education in the country. The institutions and programmes are important in inserting Kenya's presence and contribution into the global knowledge economy. This is possible if the institutions and programmes are founded on missions that integrate a vision of social responsibility and research into their operations. The drive for the privatisation of higher education and the growth of private university institutions have not developed out of a policy context initiated by Kenya. Public universities were forced to privatise their programmes largely through structural adjustment measures imposed by donors. These measures reduced the share of government subsidies going to higher education, and forced university administrators to admit private students who pay full tuition fees to generate money to run the universities. The public universities also integrated a business model into the conventional mission of the university to run most of their programmes profitably. Universities for their part have taken time to formulate policies that guide the operation of the private programmes. Strikes over the distribution of income from the programmes between lecturers and non-teaching employees in all the public universities continued during the period of this study. Financial and administrative governance of the programmes has also created tension in all the universities. Issues related to student admissions versus their academic profiles, teaching and assessment have occasionally fuelled student riots.

The private universities have been established in the same context. Globalisation, as the ideological project of economic liberalisation, opened most sectors that were previously dominated by public provision, to private providers. This coupled with increasing demand for higher education forced Kenya to start the process of chartering private universities. The issue of expanding access to higher education was however one that the government had always wanted to pursue. By the 1990s, the thinking within government policy circles was that such expansion should be undertaken with strict government regulation, and in any case through the public university system. In this respect, under the universities investment project (UIP) proposals of 1990, the promotion of private universities was supposed to complement expansion that was to take place in the public universities (Wandiga 1997). The privatisation of public universities and the promotion of private universities were therefore supposed to meet targets that government wanted to achieve through higher education, that is, expand access while addressing equity issues, and improve quality through research and teaching. Any assessment of the challenges and prospects for private higher education should therefore gauge the extent to which privatisation and private universities have addressed the above concerns. This section briefly recasts some of the challenges private higher education in Kenya has to overcome to facilitate its growth and expansion. The prospects that would facilitate this expansion are pointed out.

Private Higher Education and Equity Considerations

The demand for access to university education in Kenya is still enormous. About sixty percent of students who qualify for university entrance are not obtaining places either in public or private universities. There are also many working Kenyans who missed their first chance of university education and are in need of second chance admission. The increasing demand for higher education from all social groups reflects the influence of economic and political globalisation that is going to be around for some time. The option for developing countries like Kenya is therefore to expand higher education and strike a balance between increased access with the research and service mission of the universities. Both public and private university institutions will have to do these to be relevant as contributors to the global knowledge economy.

Data analysis for this study shows that private universities and programmes in public universities have considerably increased access to higher education for a group of students who would otherwise have been shut out by the rigid admission regulations of public universities. In so doing, some pressure has been taken off the government in terms of financing expansion of higher education. However, the role that privatisation and private higher education institutions have played in addressing equity objectives should be analysed in a broader perspective. This is not to demean the role of private higher education. Rather the intention is to identify existing challenges and seek to marry the goals of private higher education providers with the aspirations of the society in which they operate. Opening access to students from all social groups and increasing the share of qualified students admitted to private university institutions are key challenges that private higher education in Kenya has to address.

Conclusion

As the field data in Section Three of this study show, private universities and programmes in Kenya have opened a second alternative to students from the middle and upper social classes that were always certain to access it, either locally or abroad. Rarely have they offered a first chance to students from low socioeconomic backgrounds who are excluded by financial limitations from accessing higher education. The private universities operate student financial aid schemes, but the schemes target those who have already registered. Their 'needy' situation is therefore a question of fractional differences among students who already have some financial capacity. Those who are poor do not have a chance if they cannot raise tuition fees for initial registration before they are considered for any financial aid. Private higher education institutions have not integrated equity policies into their operations. The perceptions about private universities are that they are institutions that target students from elite backgrounds. There are no efforts made to distribute access among social groups. The profile of most students in private universities lacks diversity. This presents a contradiction of sorts. In the context of the globalisation logic upon which private higher education has been founded, diversity is supposed to be a key factor and measure of their quality. By concentrating opportunities on those who are able to pay, private higher education will increasingly accentuate socioeconomic differences in Kenyan society, thus negating most indicators of social development.

The second consideration should be the extent to which access has actually been provided to the greatest number of students who qualify. Again, data presented in this study show a slow expansion of capacity in private universities. For example, in the academic year 1999–2000, public universities accommodated about 84 percent of all students enrolled in universities, while private universities accounted for only 16 percent. In the 2001–2002 academic year, public universities increased their share to 86 percent, while the share of private universities dropped to 14 percent. The percentage share remained the same in the 2003–2004 academic year. The percentage increase of new students to private universities has averaged from three to four percent over the years. Not that one expected private universities to overtake public ones in terms of numbers given their wide differences in terms of histories and missions. However, private universities entered the scene when public universities were near collapse. For some time before the public universities started privatising, private universities largely monopolised the market for students who could not gain admission to public universities. The continued unmet demand for higher education in the country should also be taken as an opportunity for the private universities to increase their capacities. However, private universities lost this opportunity to public universities, who relaxed their admission requirements, set up new campuses, and started admitting private full tuition fee-paying students. This scenario partly explains the stagnation in admission and expansion of private universities.

Private universities in Kenya count the admission of more female students as one area in which they have excelled. However, a rereading of the data in this study shows that this claim has not been a consequence of any affirmative action policy designed by the institutions. The number of female students registered in private universities is a small fraction of the total population of female students who qualify for university admission. In addition, female students are registered in academic programmes that traditionally have been labelled 'female options'. Private universities in this respect have accentuated gender inequities in access to key professional disciplines. This compares unfavourably with the private programmes of public universities where more women are accessing professional courses such as medicine and law. At the University of Nairobi, the percentage of women registered in these professional areas is higher than those in the regular programmes. In the MBA private programmes, 45 percent of students were women while in the faculty of medicine the number of female students was slightly over 50 percent (CHE 2003).

The issues raised above again present certain contradictions about the operation of private higher education institutions in Kenya related to equity. The first relates to their status as demand-absorbing institutions. Literature on the growth of private higher education in developing countries cites their existence as testimony to their capacity to absorb excess demand for higher education (Eisemon 1992, Levy 1986, Geiger 1986). In this respect, private higher education is a complement and in some respects a replacement for public higher education. Private higher education in Kenya has not however expanded adequately to respond to this challenge. The expectation was that there would have been more students registered in private universities compared to those in the public and private programmes of public universities. The reverse however is the case in Kenya. This creates a real possibility of the public higher education system taking the lead in providing private higher education.

A related issue concerns the legal status of private universities as for-profit and not-for-profit institutions. These categorisations should have a bearing on the costing of the services in the institutions and the implied affordability and equity. Irrespective of the category, private universities in Kenya charge fees within the same range. The not-for-profit institutions quote tuition fees below those of the for-profits, but institute a range of other mandatory charges that raise the cost of their programmes considerably. Irrespective of their categorisation, therefore, private universities in Kenya operate in a commercialised fashion that limits their responsiveness to equity concerns.

The relationship between the curricula in private universities and the national context in which the missions of the universities need to be ingrained poses another challenge to private higher education in Kenya. As profiled in Section Two of this study, most private universities in Kenya have a limited range in the curriculum. The universities have focussed on areas that do not require high capital investment and which previously were catered for by middle level vocational institutions. In so doing, the thrust of their academic programmes has avoided areas critical to national development needs. Arguments in favour of private higher education point out the potential of the sector to provide a differentiated and diverse curriculum. Institutional and programme diversity is an important consideration in the measurement of equity as it ensures individuals are enrolled in institutions and programs on merit. This diversity has not been accomplished in the Kenyan private universities system. Of the 17 private universities operating either as accredited or non-accredited, only four offer a purely secular curriculum. These are USIU, Kiriri Women's University of Science and Technology, Agha Khan and Strathmore. Other than USIU, the rest of these universities have not been fully accredited and the volume of their students and programmes is low. The rest of the institutions are religious based and their missions are aligned to their religious philosophies and traditions. Their curricula also contain a heavy dose of religious teaching. Besides, about two thirds of the institutions account for only about 16 percent of the total enrolments of students in private universities.

The results of this study reinforce the observations that markets cannot be relied to ensure equity in the provision of higher education (Varghese 2004:27). Public universities have also continued to expand their enrolment of private students more than purely private universities have done. The diversity of programmes in public universities and the integration of private students with those on public subsidy provide a stronger foundation for addressing aspects of equity in higher education. This is not only in terms of institutional diversity, but they have been able to increase the number of female students in competitive professional courses that are not available in private universities. Although this fact does not take into account students from poor socioeconomic backgrounds, it is a gain in terms of gender equity.

Private Higher Education, Research, Knowledge Production and Dissemination

The generation and transmission of knowledge through research is a critical function of universities. At a country level, research is important for industrial transformation, economic growth and for overall poverty reduction. In the global arena, and as the World Bank's (2002) report on 'Constructing knowledge societies' notes, universities have to give their societies an edge in the global knowledge economy. New knowledge generated from research is critical to social and economic development. These assertions call for universities (both public and private) to allocate more funds for research, strike a balance between their teaching and research responsibilities, give equal attention to basic and applied research, and create networks for the dissemination of results from research to influence policy making.

Private higher education in Kenya however has been more focussed on teaching almost to the exclusion of any research. Data from fieldwork and a critical analysis of the academic programmes of private universities show that the research function of the universities has been submerged by a combination of factors. The lack of established postgraduate courses, the quality of students, the orientation of lecturers and the lack of funds from the government and the private sector combine to diminish research at private and privatising public universities. Of the four private universities covered in the study, only one, CUEA, is seriously involved in some kind of research and knowledge dissemination. The University allocates various research grants to facilitate the field work of faculty members. USIU, the largest secular private university, and endowed from secular financial sources, does not make specific allocations for research and dissemination. Overall, critical research and broad social and economic needs of society have not been addressed by private universities. Their concentration has been in teaching commercial and vocational courses that enhance the career prospects of individual students, thereby providing more personal and fewer social benefits to students and society.

The other issue has to do with the level of postgraduate training. This is important if universities have to sustain a critical mass of human and social capital for purpose of research and development endeavour. Useful research is likely to come from a university that has a bias towards high quality training of postgraduate students. The privatisation of public universities in Kenya has increased the number of students registered in postgraduate programmes. However, the lack of rigorous teaching of research methodology courses has meant that they do not get an adequate exposure to fieldwork techniques required to generate new knowledge. Fieldwork has increasingly lost ground in favour of library desk reviews, and projects have replaced theses for postgraduate examination. These developments have been occasioned by the market demands that require quick alteration of a commodity to meet changing short-term trends. In this respect, desk reviews and project work have become fashionable for students who want to complete their studies quickly, and universities that want to admit more students for commercial purposes. The quality of training that such students undergo is rarely addressed.

Most postgraduate programmes are concentrated at the master's level. The development of PhD programmes at the private universities has not been prioritised. In the private programmes of public universities, the masters programmes are concentrated in commerce and business administration, education, and humanities. Competitive professional courses such as law, engineering and medicines have not attracted as many postgraduate students. The explanation for this trend was that in the competitive professional courses one is more marketable and can make money even with a bachelor's degree. In the other disciplines, since enrolments are high, more and more qualifications are required to have an edge in the market. The motivation for postgraduate training in a privatised university environment has therefore been higher monetary returns at a person level, not the quest for knowledge that may benefit the larger society.

The non-emphasis on quality postgraduate programmes in private universities has implications for a country's development paradigm. In a globalising world, new knowledge, especially scientific knowledge, is critical to social development. If the agenda for research in private universities is also privatised, then the public interest is obscured. Since developing countries like Kenya do not have a vibrant indigenous private sector, there is the danger that universities will miss their role as knowledge producers. Funding from private concerns may lead to research ventures that may not fit the goals of national development. The crisis over patents that the IAVI and KAVI occasioned at the University of Nairobi is a pointer to what is likely to happen in a largely privatised university sector. In this respect, the more higher education is privatised, the more the agenda of generating knowledge relevant to local conditions is diminished.

The alternative to privatisation of higher education will never be to offer it as a purely public concern. Purely public higher education is as inefficient to meet social needs as much as purely private higher education. However, as the cases of private programmes in public universities have shown, greater social benefits such as equity and programme diversity are better addressed through public universities. The likely scenario is that private higher education in Kenya is going to expand through the public university sector. This does not diminish the independent existence of private universities. However, the direction of growth would see a trend towards more public-private partnerships than private-public partnerships. Real prospects for the expansion of private higher education exist in Kenya. On the demand side, the market continues to grow. About 300,000 students qualify annually from high school to go to university. The public and private universities admit about three percent of these students. There is therefore a huge untapped market. One issue that the CHE may have to decide on relates to the need of chartering more private universities of low capacity or looking for strategies of assisting the existing institutions to expand their capacities first. On the supply side, the government continues to provide incentives for the expansion of private universities and programmes. The CHE has been given more regulatory and accreditation powers. The operations of middle level colleges that wish to twin their programmes with overseas universities have been brought under CHE. This will ease the issue of credit transfers and the recognition of qualifications that have hindered student mobility between institutions in the past. These arrangements have the potential to reduce the cost of some degree level programmes and enhance equity, especially for second-generation students. Lastly, reforms in the student loan scheme have allowed students in private universities to benefit from the government tuition loans unlike before. The government has also continued to cap the annual intake of students, whose tuition and other expenses in public universities are subsidised, at a total of 10,000. All these create prospects for enhanced student choice and enablement to take up university education in either public or private universities. The challenge is for the private university sector to tune their programmes to meet both national and international expectations.

Conclusions

The challenges that confront the growth of private higher education in Kenya relate to their limited capacities in terms of both student profiles and diversity of courses. The limitations mean that the share of students who access private higher education is smaller in comparison to demand. The focus of the private higher education institutions has been on those students who can afford their charges. In the overall perspective, the operation of private universities and programmes has not integrated equity policies that are increasingly contributing to the determination of the quality of institutions and programmes. The institutions and programmes have also focussed on teaching to the exclusion of research.

References

Aina, Tade A., 1997, 'Globalization and Social Policy in Africa: Issues and Research directions', CODESRIA Working Paper Series, No. 196, Dakar: CODESRIA.

Ajayi, J. F. Ade, Goma, L. K. H., & Johnson, Amphah, G., 1996, *The African Experience with Higher Education*. Accra, Ghana/London: AAU/James Currey & Athens.

Altbach, Philip, G., 2004, 'Globalization and the University: Myths and Realities in an unequal World', *Tertiary Education and Management*, No 1.

Altbach, Philip, G., 2001, 'Higher Education and the WTO: Globalization Run Amok', *International Higher Education*, No. 3, Spring.

Altbach, Philip, G., 1992, 'Patterns in Higher Education Development: Towards the year 2000', in *Emergent issues in comparative education*, edited by Robert, F. A., Philip, G. A & Gail, P. K, New York: State University of New York Press.

Apple, M., 2001, *Educating the Right Way*, New York: Routledge.

Apple, M., 1993, *Official Knowledge: Democratic Education in a Conservative age*, New York and London: Routledge.

Aspen Institute, 1999, *The International Poverty Gap. Investing in people and technology to build sustainable pathways out*, A report of the Aspen Institute International Peace Security and Prosperity Program, Atlanta, Georgia.

Banya, K. ,2002, 'Higher Education and the Impact of Globalization on University Education in Sub Saharan Africa', *Society for Research into Higher Education News*, No. 48.

Bok, D., 2003, *Universities in the Marketplace. The commercialization of Higher Education*, Princeton, New Jersey: Princeton University Press.

Carpenter, J., 2003, 'New Evangelical Universities: Cogs in a World System or Players in a New Game?', *International Journal of Frontier Missions*, 20, 2, Summer.

Chacha Nyaigotti-Chacha, 2002, 'Public Universities, private funding: The challenges in East Africa', Paper presented at the international symposium on African Universities in the 21st Century.

Chachage, C. L. S., 2001, 'Higher Education Transformation and Academic Exterminism', *CODESRIA Bulletin*, No. 1&2.

D'Souza Alba C., 2001, 'Reforming University Finance in Sub-Saharan Africa: A Case study of Kenya', Stanford, CA., Unpublished Ph.D. Dissertation: Stanford University.

Daystar University website, http://www.daystarus.org/history.htm

Deloitte & Touche, 1994, 'Private University study for the commission for Higher Education', Final Report. Nairobi: Kenya.

Denzin, K., 1998, 'Gender, Power and Contestation: Rethinking, Bargaining with Patriarchy', in Jackson, C. & Pearson, R., eds., *Feminist Visions of Development*, London & New York: Routledge.

Dill, D., 1997, 'Higher Education Markets and Public Policy', *Higher Education Policy*, Vol. 10, 314, pp. 167-186.

Dima, Ana-Maria, 2004, 'Higher Education Privatization in a Steering Conceptual Context', CHEPS, Twente University, Summer School: The Netherlands.

Douglass, J. A., 2005, 'All Globalization is Local: Countervailing forces and the influence on Higher Education Markets', Research and Occasional Paper Series, Centre for Studies in Higher Education, Berkeley: University of California.

East African Standard, 2004, 'Education has come full circle', 18 April.

East African Standard, 2005, 'Varsities have stopped Researching, says minister', 18 February.

East African Standard, 2005, 'Schools and Careers', 30 November.

Eisemon, T. O., 1992, 'Private Initiatives and Traditions of State Control in Higher Education in Sub-Saharan Africa', PHEE Background Paper Series, Education and Employment Division, Population and Human Resource Department, Washington DC: The World Bank.

Farrell, J. P., 1992, 'Conceptualizing Education and the Drive for Social Equality', in Robert, F. A., Philip. G. A. & Gail, P. K., eds.,. *Emergent Issues in Comparative Education*, New York: State University of New York Press, pp. 107-122.

Geiger, R. L., 1986, *Private Sectors in Higher Education; Structure, Function and Change in Eight Countries*. Ann Arbor, MI: University of Michigan Press.

Griffin, R & A. R. Khan, 1992, *Globalization and the Developing World: An essay on the international dimension of development in the post-cold war era*, Geneva: UNRISD.

Johnston, D. B., 2000, 'Privatization in and of Higher Education in the USA', Sunny-Buffalo website,

Kezar, A., 2004, 'Obtaining Integrity? Reviewing and Examining the Charter between Higher Education and Society', *The Review of Higher Education*, Vol. 27 (4), pp. 429-459.

Kiamba, C., 2003, 'The Experience of Privately Sponsored Students and Other Income Generating Activities at the University of Nairobi', Case study prepared for the Regional Training Conference on Improving Tertiary Education in Sub-Saharan Africa: Things that Work!, Accra: September 23-25.

Knight, J., 2003, 'GATS, Trade and Higher Education; perspective 2003 — where are we?', The Observatory on Borderless Higher Education Report, International Strategic Information Service.

Kwiek, M., 2003, 'The State, the Market and Higher Education; Challenges for the New Century', in *The University, Globalization Central Europe*, Kwiek Marek, ed., Frankfurt/New York: Peter Lang.

Levy, D. C., 2003, 'Profits and Practicality; How South Africa Epitomizes the Global Surge in Commercial Private Higher Education', Working Paper No 4, PROPHE, Albany State University of New York.

Levy, D. C., 1986, *Higher Education and the State in Latin America; Private Challenges to Public Dominance*, Chicago: University of Chicago Press.

Mamdani, M., 1993, 'University Crisis and University Reform: A Reflection on the African Experience', *CODESRIA Bulletin*, No. 3.

References

Miriam, H., 2001, 'Policy Approaches to Educational Disadvantage and Equity in Australian Schooling', International Institute for Educational Planning Working Document, Paris.

Mkandawire, T., 1998, 'Notes on Consultancy and Research in Africa', Copenhagen: Centre for Development Research.

Mohamedbhai, G., 1998, *The Role of Higher Education in Developing a Culture of Peace in Africa: Achievements, Challenges and Prospects*, UNESCO, Regional Office for Education in Africa, Dakar: UNESCO.

Murunga, G. R., 2001, 'Private Universities in the Kenya Higher Education Experience', *CODESRIA Bulletin*, No. 1 & 2.

Mwiria, K, & Ngome, C. K., 1998, 'The World of Private Universities; the Experience of Kenya', *NORRAG NEWS*. No. 23, October.

Newman, F., 2000, 'Saving Higher Education's Soul', www.Futures.project.org

Nisbet, R., 1971, *The Degradation of the Academic Dogma: The University in America, 1945–1970*, New York: Basic Books.

Ntshoe, I. M., 2003, 'Higher Education and Training Policy and Practice in South Africa: Impacts of Global Privatization, quasi-Marketization and new Managerialism', *International Journal of Educational Development* (24), pp. 137-154.

Olukoshi, A. & Oyekanmi, F., 2001, 'Editorial', *CODESRIA Bulletin*. Nos. 1& 2, Dakar: CODESRIA.

Reehana, R., n.d., 'Ensuring Access and Equity through Measuring', International Research Foundation for Open Learning, Cambridge, http://www.ignou.ac.in/theme

Republic of Kenya, 2004, 'Kenya Review and Appraisal: Final Report on the implementation of Beijing Platform for Action, 1994-2004'.

Republic of Kenya, 2003, *Economic Survey*, Nairobi: Government Printer.

Republic of Kenya., 1991, Ministry of Education, *University Education in Kenya, Request for World Bank Credit*, Nairobi: Government Printer.

Republic of Kenya, 1981, *Report of the Presidential Working Party on the Establishment of the Second University in Kenya*, Nairobi: Government Printer.

Rhoades, G., n.d., 'Democracy and Capitalism Academic Style: Governance in contemporary Higher Education'.

Ross, M. G., 1976, *The University; The anatomy of academy*, McGraw Hill Books Company.

Saint, W. S., 1992, *Universities in Africa; Strategies for Stabilization and Revitalization*, Washington DC: The World Bank.

Samoff, J. and Bidemi, C., 2003, 'From Manpower Planning to the Knowledge Era: World Bank Policies on Higher Education in Africa', UNESCO Forum, Occasional Paper Series, No. 2, Stanford University.

Shafritz, J, M and Russell, E. W., 2000, *Introducing Public Administration*, 2nd edition, Addison Wesley Longman.

Spartains Educational, 2001, 'Women in the University', www.spartacus.schoolnet.co.uk

Teffera, D. & Altbach, P. G., eds., 2003, *African Higher Education; An International Reference Handbook*, Bloomington: Indiana University Press.

UNESCO, 2004, 'Gender and Education for All: The Leap to Equity', in *Global Monitoring Report 2003/04*, http://portal.unesco.org/education

UNESCO, 1998, *World Declaration on Higher Education in the 21st Century, Vision and Action, and Framework for Priority, Action for change and Development in Higher Education*, Paris, October.

UNESCO, 1993, *World Education Report*, Paris: UNESCO.

University of Nairobi, 2003, 'Graduation booklet'.

USIU, 2005, 'Data Elements (DE) to support the capacity and preparatory Review, Report', Nairobi, USIU.

Varghese, N. V., 2004, 'Private Higher Education in Africa', International Institute for Educational Planning, Association for the Development of Education in Africa and the Association of African Universities.

Wandiga, S.O., 1997, *Capacity Building and Institutional Development in Higher Education in Kenya*, Paris: UNESCO, IIEP.

Williamson, J., 1999, 'What Should the Bank Think about the Washington Consensus?', Paper prepared for the World Bank's World Development Report, 2000, Washington DC: The World Bank.

World Bank, 2004, 'Focus on Women and Development', in Devnews Media Centre, www.worldbank.org/wbsite/external/news.

World Bank, 2002, *Constructing Knowledge Societies; New Challenges for Higher Education*, Washington DC: The World Bank.

World Bank, 2000, *Higher Education in Developing Countries: Peril and Promise*, The Task Force on Higher Education and Society, Washington DC: The World Bank.

World Bank, 1995, *Towards Gender Equity, The Role of Public Policy*, Washington DC: The World Bank.

World Bank, 1987, *Education in Sub-Saharan Africa. Policies for Adjustment, Revitalization and Expansion*, Washington DC: The World Bank.

Zeleza, P. T., 2003, 'Academic Freedom in the Neo-liberal Order; Governments, Globalization, Governance and Gender', *Journal of Higher Education in Africa*, Vol. 1, No. 1, pp. 149–194.